LOVE JUNKIE

RACHEL RESNICK is the author of *Los Angeles Times* best-seller, *Go West Young F*cked-Up Chick*. She has published articles, essays and celebrity-profile cover stories in the *Los Angeles Times*, *Women's Health*, and *BlackBook*. She is a contributing editor at *Tin House* magazine. Her essays and stories have also appeared in *The Time of My Life*, *Damage Control*, *The Dictionary of Failed Relationships*, *The Best American Erotica 2004*, *Women on the Edge*, *L.A. Shorts* and *Absolute Disaster*. She is the founder and CEO of Writers on Fire, provider of luxury writing retreats both in the United States and abroad.

LOVE JUNKIE

A MEMOIR

Rachel Resnick

BLOOMSBURY

LONDON · BERLIN · NEW YORK

B RES

Author's note: Some of the names, locations and details of events in this book have been changed to protect the privacy of persons involved.

First published in Great Britain 2009
This paperback edition published 2010

Bloomsbury Publishing, London, Berlin and New York

36 Soho Square, London W1D 3QY

A CIP catalogue record for this book is available from the British Library

ISBN 9781408801178

10 9 8 7 6 5 4 3 2 1

Typeset by Hewer Text UK Ltd, Edinburgh
Printed in Great Britain by Clays Ltd, St. Ives plc

Mixed Sources
Product group from well-managed
forests and other controlled sources
www.fsc.org Cert no. SGS-COC-2061
© 1996 Forest Stewardship Council
FSC

www.bloomsbury.com/rachelresnick

To my brother

CHAPTER ONE

Problems with Rachel

2006

On Observation Drive, the narrow street where I have lived for eight years, I back the cherry red metallic pickup truck down the steep driveway toward my home, navigate past a startled raccoon, which drops a discarded can of refried beans it's pried from the garbage. Just then Jim Morrison starts singing "The End." I sing along the way I never do in front of anyone. There's always a Doors song on a radio station somewhere on the dial in Los Angeles. After it's over I cut the engine, listen to the ticking, pause before gaining the comfort of my tiny one-bedroom hideaway. My sanctuary. Since I took a little break from dating men a year ago, I've grown to relish the solitude and the peace.

I always feel lucky when I get home.

But as soon as I set foot in the door, I know something's wrong. Ajax, the homicidal scarlet macaw I rescued four years before, is uncharacteristically quiet.

"Ajax, you okay?"

Ajax stalks the fancy stainless steel "animal environment" that serves as his cage, ruffles up his neck feathers, glares. His pupils are flaring, like he's pissed. That's not something you like to see in your scarlet macaw. He has the power to snap your finger in two, or bite through phone cords, which he likes to do for fun when he's out of the cage.

I walk into my bedroom. At first I can't locate the source of my unease. The bookcases are fine, the yellow tulips are still neatly arranged in a vase on the desk. There is the dashboard Hula Man from Hawaii, my desk mascot, next to the miniature Ganesh. On the wall, the painting by the Sandman, the Alabama outsider artist, and next to it the framed black-and-white snapshot of my mother, who died when I was fourteen, looking eternally young and bright-eyed in her high school photo. Nothing's out of place.

Then I notice the darkened computer. Inside are years of e-mails—including the thousands I exchanged with Spencer, my most recent boyfriend and quasi-fiancé, over the ten months we were together—along with all the stories I've written, my second novel, the new novel, all the teaching exchanges, everything. The computer's green eye is not blinking. The computer, from which I generate my very living, is dead.

For a moment, I stop breathing. Blink. This can't be happening.

"Ajax," I call out softly, disoriented. I hear him stretch his wings in response.

Then my brain starts racing. Maybe there was a power outage. Those things happen in the canyon. I drop to my knees, edge close. Startled, I pull back my hand from the carpet where the hard drive sits. It's completely soaked.

Was there a sudden rainstorm? Canyon weather can be unpredictable. I move my hands closer to the wall, check for drips from the window. Nothing. Maybe something leaked from my landlord's home upstairs? It's happened before. No sign of that either. Besides, the computer hard drive sits under a sturdy desk fashioned from a door set on two filing cabinets. The only water anywhere is concentrated in a thick wet pool right beneath the hard drive. It makes no sense.

Then I see a bead of water leak from the interior of the drive, squeeze through the disk portal, and drip slowly down the plastic.

The computer was a gift from Spencer.

And tonight is the night before Valentine's Day.

And it hits me suddenly: Spencer did this. Drowning my computer is the perfect fuck-you Valentine. I cup my hand over my mouth, muzzle the horror. It might as well be blood leaking from the hard drive. Water poured directly into a computer instantly short-circuits the whole system, erasing all data.

Let me translate what this means to me at this moment in my life.

After decades of chasing love and ignoring the reality of my own life, I am worn to a nub. My nerves are raw. My body and heart ache. My bank account is empty—wait, that's not quite right. It's actually overdrawn. On top of which, I owe Spencer money. Everything is so fragile and tenuous that this violation could send me over the edge. The memory of this period fills me with shame, because I created the calamitous circumstances.

I can't afford any physical accidents or technical mishaps.

Nor can I afford to lose the data the computer holds. What it means to me.

Let me try to explain.

The computer is a living extension of my brain, an expression of my soul, a museum of my fragmented life. It is how I connect with my friends, how I process my thoughts, where I stash memories, where I recount dreams and stories, in a matrix of files. It's also the only place where an overdue decent-paying magazine article exists, not to mention the nearly finished book manuscript I was planning to sell.

To attack it is to attack me. To destroy it is to destroy me.

I know this sounds extreme. Unfortunately, at this point in my life, it's the truth.

My gaze jerks to the window. The blinds are bunched up, like someone took them in the palm of their hand and crushed them. I can feel my heart pounding, beating against the cage of ribs. On the carpet, boot marks. A man's size. The bird remains unusually silent. Normally he's laughing his avian head off, or saying repeatedly, "Hello! Hello?" in various tones, to which I parry with a call and response that somehow I never get tired of doing. Maybe it's shame that holds his black piston of a tongue, shame because he failed to protect his domain. Because clearly, judging from the crumpled blinds and the boot marks, someone has come through the window.

I run to the cage, panicking. Spencer always hated Ajax.

"It's okay, Ajax, it's okay. I love you. Are you okay? Did he try to poison you? Do you need to go to the vet? Tell me, handsome."

Ajax's feathers smooth out. He cocks his head, studying me. He seems fine now. But is he in danger? Spencer could come back. Next time . . . unless—a nerve-prickling thought comes to me. Unless he's still here.

Without thinking, I look for a weapon. Pick up a kitchen knife. Listen for movement. I force myself to check behind each door, in each hiding place, but the apartment is small, only two rooms and a bathroom—three, if you count the little walk-in dressing area. The kitchen morphs into a living space; the bedroom also serves as the office and library. Actually, there are books and bookcases in every room, even the bathroom. There's really nowhere to hide, unless you're a book or a squirrel.

He's not here.

Still shaking, I pick up the phone.

"Stasia, call me back. I know it's late. I'm sorry to call so late. I hope I didn't wake you and the kids. But it's an emergency. Spencer broke into my house and wrecked my computer. You've got to call me back."

Anastasia and I have been friends since right after college, when we were both living in Rome. For years we were hellions together, plowing through men, running around town—until she got married and had two kids. Now I barely see her. She's busy, lives on the other side of town, but we still talk every day. She's family.

Then I call Samantha, my friend who lives up the road in Topanga Canyon in a trailer, the Cowgirl Palace. More family. The women who never let you down. Sam picks up right away. I don't even remember what I say.

5

"You want me to come over? Spend the night?" she says. "What a fucking psycho."

Her words comfort me, though there's a dull nagging thought—who's psycho? I picked him. I kept him. I kept him even after he began debasing me, just as I picked and kept a lifetime of other men who seduced and then debased. So if he's psycho, aren't I psycho too?

There's no way to dress this up either and make myself look good in the process.

This is a story about my years of compulsive sex, romantic obsession, the endless demeaning e-mails I wrote, the addictive relationships I pursued—convinced each man was, in fact, the love of my life—and the time and effort wasted. It's also a story about how I finally decided to break the cycle, and how I slipped, and how I tried to find my way again.

What does it cost when someone asks you to marry them—three times—and backs out—three times? A dollar? A year's rent? A trip around the world? What does it cost when that same man chips away at your self-esteem, with lists of criticisms? And you stick it out because you think this might be your last chance to have it all—a husband, a child of your own—before it's too late? Does that add up to ten thousand, a hundred thousand, a quarter million in damages?

I owe Spencer a thousand dollars. Maybe he thinks demolishing the computer is a kind of justice. I remember he once punctured all four tires of a man's car after the man parked in his spot too many times. If he only knew I had the check to pay him back, in full, right here on the desk ready to send. With money borrowed from my brother.

What kind of sick cosmic joke is this? Isn't humor all about timing? I can't help but smile, however grimly. My humor has always saved me, or at least softened the blows. Maybe I was meant to face the wreckage of my past, the consequences of my choices and stubborn clinging. Maybe God thinks I need to be slapped upside the head to truly wake up.

I'm a freelance writer, always struggling month to month to pay basic bills, juggling credit to cover the gaps. I'm doing the best I can. I tried to pay Spencer back whenever I got a chance, even in small payments, but recently I'd struggled just to pay the landlord. I remember how Spencer thought that I was a successful writer at first, that I owned a house, had assets and investments, and how disappointed he was when he found out that wasn't the case.

It started like a fairy tale.

When Spencer and I first met at Moonshadows in Malibu, after flirting on Nerve.com for one day, we couldn't stop talking. There in the outdoor Blue Lounge, we drank vodka tonics and smoked Sobranie Black Russian cigarettes while the gulls and the hours floated by on the moon-dappled ocean below.

"Let's play the Freakout Game," he said. "What if I told you I'd been waiting to meet you my whole life?"

After three days, he e-mailed me a coupon that read

Rachel Miranda Resnick,
  I would rather die than add one more ounce of heartache
  and pain and disappointment to your life.
  Spencer Wozniak

"Print it out," he said. If I had, maybe this story would be different. But I doubt it.

In the beginning, Spencer was perfection. Though he looked menacing with his wide-set blue eyes, shaved head, and steroidal physique, he was the biggest teddy bear: an amateur chef who cooked me gourmet meals every night and invented desserts like Rachel's Kiss (strawberries dipped in Frangelico fudge on amaretto-infused vanilla ice cream) and dishes like Ceviche Confetti (sea scallops marinated in roasted tomatillos, papaya, lime juice, and Serrano chiles on a bed of radicchio); who gave me my own fancy Italian cappuccino maker and brought me perfect cappuccinos in bed with fresh-cut mango; who flew me out to meet his Polish immigrant parents in Phoenix the first month; and who made love to me multiple times a day, always making sure I was satisfied, and whose gloriously uncircumcised cock with its hooded charms and textured driving power inspired worship.

Here was this guy striking enough to have scored bit parts in a few cult indie films and a scattering of thuggish music videos; a seasoned street fighter who earned a semiotics degree at Reed College, and wrote the Reed newspaper's weekly sex advice column in the guise of a woman; who loved my writing and told me so; who showered compliments; who said he wanted me; who promised that we would travel the world, make a family—and who always had a good bottle of champagne in the fridge.

Who could blame me for staying when he first pointed out a tiny flaw in me? After all, I am well aware of being deeply flawed.

"You have a tendency to be late. Especially when we have a date to be somewhere. Maybe you should make a list each day and calculate the exact time each part requires."

I furrowed my brow, grabbed the yellow legal pad I used to scribble daily lists of things to do. The day's page was already chaotic and crowded with tasks, calls, Post-its, exclamation points. Some items were months old, still undone. I reread Spencer's e-mail. Then I tried to mark each task with an estimated time, each effort a tiny hammer tapping on my skull. The hammers gathered speed. I wasn't sure whether the times I chose were reasonable, whether I could even do any of the tasks, or why I felt so out of control. All I knew was that as I calculated, numbers seemed to fray at the edges, unravel, then sift senselessly to the floor.

I e-mailed Spencer back in defeat: "I'm trying. I can't do it. Please help."

The phone calls, conversations, and e-mails gradually took on an increasingly scolding tone. Things like, "Maybe being so expressive about sex could be construed as bullying," or, "Why are you so moody?" Or, "You don't answer questions, you're squirrelly."

Almost imperceptibly, the exchanges turned harsher:

"Do you ever do ANYTHING in the moment besides complain about the past or recent past?"

I was terrified he was cutting me off. He turned cold. But once I fall, I'm done. As Stasia says about me and men, "You're like a dog with a bone." Over the past two decades, she's seen how I cling way past the point of ugliness.

Meanwhile, I began missing deadlines—for teaching, for writing. I was barely hanging on. I began racking up serious credit card debt.

He continued his harangue: "Every single little thing is an opportunity for more grief and conflict and strife when placed in your over-reactive, over-sensitive hands. You have transformed my once pretty happy and peaceful world, on the whole, into a minefield, with the occasional wonderful, lovely time for variety's sake. Thanks."

I was trying desperately to please him, or at worst, argue him out of his harsh criticisms. The word "minefield" sent me spinning off into days of self-examination, soul-searching, beating myself up. Friends grew tired of my ramblings. Their advice to just get out fell on deaf ears.

My first *Los Angeles Times* assignment lay dormant. The editor's queries unanswered. It appeared every day on my list of things to do, neglected. My book agent couldn't reach me. My teaching suffered. I lost students. My job was to make sure this relationship worked. At all costs. If it took fifty e-mails of justifications and explanations, late-night drive-overs and I'm-sorry blow jobs, sign me up. Spencer might as well have been heroin. Everything was falling apart.

"You have single-handedly allowed your mood swings and your profound insecurities and your deep depression to tear apart what had been a very lovely young relationship. You saw that. Saw it clearly. But have not taken strong enough measures to lessen the damage you have caused."

Finally the criticisms bloomed into a meticulously detailed, twenty-page numbered list printed out for my edification.

Granted, he called them our "issues" and attempted to balance these out with "constructive" ways to overcome them—but in truth, they were a series of complaints about my character. Originally he delivered them verbally, presented as problems he had with me that I needed to address or else we couldn't continue the relationship. Then they appeared in e-mail form. There were so many e-mails, so many criticisms. Sometimes stand-alone, sometimes embedded in niceties. I still remember the folded pages, how I carried them around with me, unable to keep track of my flaws without referring to them. My friends and I began calling them "Problems with Rachel." We laughed about it, in that black comic kind of way. These brief periods of relief kept me going. I talked about those Problems as a kind of sucker punch to the gut. What I didn't share with my friends was that they were also a kind of relief. Spencer saw me. Saw me as I truly was: a demon hiding in the guise of a fucked-up woman.

My friends also dared to wonder out loud how I could be such a tough woman, so independent, so powerful, and yet once again succumb to a controlling man. Was I some kind of masochist? If I was, I fed off the fighting just as much. I was always right in there, ready with a rejoinder. I kept the ugliest vision of myself to myself. And continued to curl my eyelashes, dress sexy, gussy up to keep my man.

So Spencer and I had enjoyed maybe a month of pure bliss. We fought for the next nine. Until he broke up with me for good.

Why didn't I leave?

Because that's not how it works.

Ever since my first serious boyfriend at age twenty-one, when I finally told someone "I love you" and fell down the romantic rabbit hole, this pattern has emerged and placed a shadowy choke hold on all my subsequent love relationships.

Maybe I suspect I'm dark, and rotten, and unworthy. Possibly I need to be swept up and seduced, obsessed over, then degraded. Built up, then shattered. Why, I do not know. But ever since Spencer, the most devastating relationship I've yet been in and the one that constituted "hitting rock bottom," I've taken a temporary vow of celibacy so I can step back and try to figure it out.

What I think so far is this addiction is lethal, rooted in the most primal ground of childhood damage. And once that attachment has set in, shaking it is tantamount to weaning oneself off the most addictive and powerful drugs.

This book is my journey through a lifelong pattern of ruinous relationships with men, a pattern that may have cost me my chance to have a child, or a healthy relationship of any kind. It's my attempt to understand, and end, a pattern that has been yielding worse and worse choices. Before I can even begin to explore that pattern, though, the real question is, what is wrong with me?

CHAPTER TWO
The Blue Flame

1974

My mother cried over all the men in her life.

I am in the Blue Flame, a dive bar in Onset, Massachusetts, carefully folding a dollar bill. This bar's okay because the bartender's nice and there's a good jukebox. Right now it's playing "Fire" by the Ohio Players, which is one of the first 45s I ever bought. It's still pretty early, so the smoke isn't too bad. Still, whenever I need to inhale deeply, I bring a napkin to my mouth, breathe through it. I'm in sixth grade, eleven years old. I do not want to get cancer.

Inside the bar, the air is thick with the smell of stale beer and dirty dishrags and something I sense but won't recognize for another decade: low-rent despair. There's barely any light. I've commandeered my own red citronella candle with the white plastic netting so I can see what I'm doing. On the back of the bar is a lit-up 3-D picture of a waterfall with a green beer bottle sliding down; somehow the frosty white-blue lights flicker in such a way it looks like the water is really falling. It's pretty cool, but not after you've stared at it for what feels like hours. At least I have a new project now.

First I wipe away any liquid and crumbs, lay the dollar bill out flat on the least sticky part of the wood. Then I fold it lengthwise, like an accordion, so you can still see the pyramid with the eye. I make sure to bend the part with the pyramid and eye around so I can fit it into the band. Then I fold the long part into a ring, slip it into a fold so it's secure, and presto, I have a dollar-bill ring! The pyramid and eye are right on top, just like the man showed me. Perfect. I slip it on my right index finger.

"Hey!" I say, tapping the skinny man who taught me how to do this on the back—he's only one stool over. He turns slightly, looks at me like he doesn't know me, even though he spent a whole half hour only a little while ago showing me how to make this dollar-bill ring. When he demonstrated, I counted how many buttons he had unbuttoned on his shirt—four. Enough so you could see where the dog tags on the silver chain hit the part of his chest that divides into two muscles, and I could tell he really did used to be a wrestler, like he said. Now his eyes are glassy big and kind of haunted, just like my mother's. Drunk eyes.

I lean around him and say really loudly, "Ma! Look at the ring I made!"

I extend my bedollared finger. My mother glances my way, but her gaze drifts off the ring and onto the far wall.

"When're we eating dinner? I'm starving."

"A few minutes, Rachel," she whispers. "Can't you see I'm busy? Have another Slim Jim."

"We've been here since school." I look at the Miller Time clock, with the pretty beer-gold neon frame. "It's almost six."

"I'm talking to someone right now," she hisses, her pale blue eyes narrowing. When she gets this drunk, her eyes turn into cold blue ice floes. Witchy. No way can I do a stare-down like she always dares me to do when she's like this. I swivel on my bar stool, turn my back to them, take the ring apart, and start over.

After refolding the ring about ten thousand times, I start writing Do Not Smoke warnings on a stack of paper place mats the bartender gives me. He lends me a pen too. Then I go around the bar, handing them out. I make sure to smile when I'm doing it because I think that's a more effective way of getting my message across. Everyone seems to get a kick out of the place mats, especially the little cartoons I draw of the people.

"Is that me?" asks one woman, pointing. Her hair is in a really high beehive, her body like a sack of potatoes stuffed into a shiny green polyester top. Her eye shadow is green too, and her eyelashes are long and fake. I like the way she laughs. I thought I made her look a lot better than she really does. I didn't draw all her fat parts.

"You're a little devil, aren't you!" she says, grabbing hold of my cheek the way adults will. "What're you doing in here, anyway? Where's your mother?"

"Please don't smoke. It's not good for your health," I say, bouncing away to another table. Some people brush me off, tell me to get lost, but I don't care. I still drop the warning on their table. It's a mission. Then I return to the bar, walk up to the stool where my mother sits.

"Ma?" I say, tugging on her loose purple T-shirt. "I have homework."

My mother waves her hand in my direction as if I'm a horsefly. It's like she's already forgotten I'm here. I'm about to tug harder when I see she's digging out her wallet from the back pocket of her jeans.

She unfolds the well-creased drawing on the bar, smoothes it out, and says to the man, extremely loudly, "Look what my daughter thinks of me."

Not again. I wish I'd never made it. I figure it's going to be another half hour, which is how long she usually cries over the drawing. I quickly scoot back to my own bar stool.

This picture, which I drew with my favorite 000 Rapidograph pen that my father bought me, shows my mother with her hair frizzed out, her potbelly swelling, her arms outstretched with a bottle of beer in one hand and a cigarette in the other. I spent a lot of time on this drawing; I even detailed the beer label in miniature—Miller, her favorite. I'd given this picture to her and asked why she didn't look like the women in Andrew Lang's *The Olive Fairy Book*—slender, with long flowing blonde hair and green eyes. "It's because you wear cowboy boots, Ma." I was just trying to help. To get her to see what was wrong, shape up, fix it. Stop drinking, stop smoking, lose weight, work out, do her hair, spend more time with me.

The truth is my mother used to be beautiful, and not many years ago either. Ever since this past summer, before I started sixth grade, she doesn't put Dippity-do in her hair—there's a big white streak in the middle and she's not even forty—she doesn't put on lipstick, she let herself get overweight, and instead of wearing those cool dashikis and elephant pants, or black turtlenecks and kilts and high heels to show off her amazing legs, like she used to, she dresses every day in jeans and a loose T-shirt and boots like some broken-down cowgirl. Except we live in Massachusetts and there aren't any horses around.

I glance over and see tears sliding down my mother's face. This makes me feel sick. I'd like to wrap my arms around her, hold her and have her hold me, I miss that, but she's so far away, and I know from years of seeing it that she wants the arms of a man. Sometimes I wonder if the tears pumping out are really beer, the drinking's so connected to the crying. The man is leaning in close now, like he's studying the caricature. He snakes his arm around my mother's waist, plants a sloppy kiss right on her quivering lips.

Like I haven't seen this before a trillion times.

I know exactly what comes next. I always do. In another hour, my mother will pull it together to drive me home in her beat-up green Ford pickup, and this man will follow behind until we get there. Then I will go to my room and slam my door shut.

First I'll hear whispers, then laughter. Some bed creaking. I will try to drown out the sounds with my radio or portable record player. The two-floor divided half of the prefab house we rent is cheap, the walls are thin. We're surviving on food stamps and handouts from my father, who left when I was four, and my mother's rich relatives.

Nobody would believe it if I told them that my mother was a proper blue blood Boston debutante, Seven Sisters–educated, that there are wooden tagged and authenticated pieces of the *Mayflower* in the attic of her parents' house, that my mother owns a quarter of this summer house we call the Big House— ten bedrooms, three stories, the whole place covered in weathered gray shingle—in Marion, down a dirt road, right on a private beach overlooking Buzzards Bay, at the gateway to Cape Cod, with a breakwater busted up by a long-ago hurricane, twenty acres including its own clay tennis court with a sagging backboard, miles of brambled woods and rocky seaweed-covered beach to explore, a hedged-in English garden and honeysuckle bushes, pine trees to climb, plenty of rooms and linen closets and cellars to hide in, a hydrangea bush and a croquet field, a foghorn you hear at night, and a barn too, so I don't bother.

Meanwhile, I ask the bartender for more ginger ale, peanuts. Without my even asking, he also slides me a bowl full of maraschinos, along with some more paper place mats. This bartender is definitely my friend. I draw him a picture for a present, and he folds it up and puts it in his shirt pocket.

An hour later we leave the Blue Flame. I don't talk to my mother as we drive home. I'm just hoping we don't crash like we have before. She and her whole side of the family have a habit of wrecking cars.

"Did you like Doug?"

"Doug," I say, like I'm eating dog doo, to show her how mad I am. Plus I make a face.

"That's a nice sour expression, daughter of mine."

The sound of empty beer bottles rattling behind the seats creates a deafening *clang-bang-clash-click-kachunk* kind of racket every time we hit a bump in the road. There must be a hundred back there. I've given up asking if they're going to be recycled. I think my mother might like the noise.

What do you know, right behind us is a rusted-out Pinto, sweeping its headlights into our cab. Doug's here. He slams the car door shut, clomps up the sidewalk in his work boots.

When we all get in the door, I see my younger brother, Michael, age three, wandering around the house alone like a lost towheaded baby ghost, dragging his "String" with one end twisted into a point and wedged firmly in his nose. String is the lining of his security blanket. The lining is all that's left. Me, I still have my security blanket, minus the lining. Mine's called "Pink" (and I have it today, although now it's gray).

"You're gross," I say. "Get that out of your nose."

Michael grins at me, shoves it in deeper.

"Was anyone watching you?"

Michael shakes his head no, his blond hair tangled and matted.

Our mother tromps upstairs with the man. He slaps her butt as they go, both of them giggling and stumbling.

I yank String out of my brother's nose, drag him into the kitchen. There are dishes stacked in the sink, thick crud on the linoleum floor, garbage strewn in various spots, spills and stains on the counters.

"Time for potpies," I say, opening the freezer. "What'll it be? Big selection, Michelob. Chicken or beef?"

We probably eat Morton potpies six nights a week, on our own.

"Don't call me 'Michelob'!" he cries.

When I get up the next morning, I'm hoping the man is gone from our home. But when I go to brush my teeth, I can hear them murmuring in the bedroom, the bed squeaking, the creepy slap of flesh and groans.

I know that they are having sexual intercourse. I've been learning a lot about it lately. Earlier this week I snuck my mother's copy of *The Happy Hooker* and read the whole thing in one night. I've also been studying her book of Japanese erotic art and the *Playboy* magazines she gives to me and my friends. When she does that, and sits there with us, picking out attractive photos, telling us it's okay, sex is normal, I don't look. I'm embarrassed. But alone I pore over these same magazines.

And now, listening to the sounds from her bedroom, I get out my sketch pad and draw a girl having sex with a boy, in graphic detail. Then I draw it again, in different ways, add more boys, another girl, until my face and body are burning with shame and I'm filled with a strange kind of excitement I don't understand at all—and then I shred every page into narrow strips so no one can tell what it is.

Afterward, I go downstairs, get Michael and me bowls of cold cereal. Pretty soon Doug comes down, enters the kitchen. He smells of sex.

All he's wearing are some ratty plaid boxers and my mother's jean jacket. His chest is pale white, wiry with muscle, hairless; he looks like B. J. Thomas on the cover of the *Raindrops Keep*

Fallin' on My Head album. My mother told me Thomas was a junkie. I don't know what that is yet, but Doug reminds me of him. In the morning light he looks really young and old at the same time. He nods at us, opens the fridge like he owns it, and pulls out a beer. Closes it. He stands there for a few minutes in front of the fridge swaying. Maybe he's thinking, or sleeping, or something. My brother and I watch him and crunch cereal. Then the man opens the fridge again, takes out another bottle. Goes back upstairs.

When he's gone, my brother lifts up his shirt, opens his eyes all woozy and spacey. We start laughing, snorting milk through our nostrils.

Before I leave, I give Michael homework for the day: "Read this book, draw me a picture of a stegosaurus, then of a giant squid, watch *Electric Company*, and memorize the alphabet."

Then I walk to the bus stop. I can't wait to get to school. Sometimes I wish I could stay at school overnight. Or live there.

Doug doesn't call again.

For the next week, I come home after school to find my mother walking around in a daze, still dressed in her see-through baby-doll nightie. If she's even up. Otherwise, she stays in bed all day, and night. Sometimes she'll cry openly, but mostly she'll just weep behind her locked bedroom door.

The week after that, every night she packs us into the car to go pick up injured animals by the side of the road. As I sit with their whimpering bloodied masses, I watch her as closely as I watch the wounded animals.

Then one day, my mother comes to pick me up at school. I pretend I don't know her, delay as long as I can, but finally I leave the jacks game behind and climb into the truck. Instead of going right home, though, my mother drives us to a new bar, Narrows Crossing, over on the Cranberry Highway.

"Only for a few minutes," she says. And I know we're starting all over.

My mother was the original love junkie. She taught me well.

The year is 2007. It is almost twelve whole months since the vandalism of my computer. After I endured a hellish week of sleepless nights and agonizing, a brilliant tech specialist managed to retrieve all my data. My brother, Michael, now thirty-five, bought me a new computer as a gift, so here I am again. Still single, still seeking answers. Still mostly abstinent, except for three slips. Thanks to a twelve-step program for love junkies, I have stayed clear of obsessive harmful relationships for more than two years.

Right now, I'm sitting at the same desk, gazing out at the familiar sun-splashed hills of Topanga State Park. A red-tailed hawk glides through the flawless sky. There's a heady scent of jasmine coming in from the deck trellis. The air is warm, even balmy. My mother would've loved this place. A ruby-throated hummingbird zooms in front of the window, whirs for a few seconds, then disappears. Earlier I did a grueling half-hour set of cliffside stairs in Santa Monica, so my legs are burning. I can't help smiling. In many respects, my life is kind of idyllic.

Before me is a simple form I must fill out in order to teach at the University of Southern California. My pulse quickens. Forms like this one are the source of recurring nightmares for me. Where did you grow up? At what schools did you study?

Where did you work? What years? Who is your emergency contact? These questions have always stumped me. They remind me of a fractured past that honestly feels like someone else's life—or many lives. I've never been able to integrate them all.

Maybe one reason I cling to documentation and data—I have trouble erasing e-mails even decades old, collect love letters, keep thousands of files—is this: I often can't remember the basic facts of my life.

I can't recall all the places I lived. I can't summon the names of the towns, cities, even the schools, there were so many. Let me see—Jerusalem, Israel; Bridgeville, Delaware; Pulaski, Tennessee; New York City; Marion, Massachusetts; Cranford, New Jersey; Sylacauga, Alabama . . . is that right? If I do remember, I can't place them in order correctly. What's the chronology? Memories come back in fragments—floating scenes, colors and sounds, snatches of dialogue—incidents cut loose from time. My own history overwhelms me.

And no one can help me reconstruct it.

I was fourteen when my mother died, twelve when she lost custody of my brother and me. My brother went to live with his father's family, and I went to live with four foster families. I am not in close touch with many of my blood relatives, who had little use for my mother and her brood. Who's got records of my past, my schools? Don't ask me what childhood illnesses I've had, or whether I've been vaccinated. I have no idea.

My mother's been dead almost thirty years. My father and I haven't spoken for two years.

*　　*　　*

My mother cried over all the men in her life. It seemed to me she was always crying.

My first memory is of my mother and me sitting in the rocking chair in the apartment on West 110th Street in Manhattan, me in her lap. I must be around three. My father has gone away. I ask my mother when Daddy is coming back.

"I don't know," she says.

Just as I'm about to cry, she starts crying. I watch the tears well up from the corners of her light blue eyes in horror. So instead of crying, I comfort her; I want to be strong. I reach out, but I can't even stretch my small arms around her.

"Don't cry, Ma. Don't cry."

The tears stream down, tracking the dirty silt of mascara like mud on her high cheekbones, until my mother is shaking and sobbing.

I am four when my parents divorce and my father leaves for good.

Then in 1970, my mother remarries. It is the summer before I start first grade. I am six years old.

My mother's second husband, Angus Mathews, is shorter than my mother but ruggedly good-looking. One hundred percent Black Irish, Angus has piercing blue eyes and wavy black hair he wears in a mullet. He's built like a brawny leprechaun.

"I met a man," she tells me, all out of breath, face flushed. She'd just been to visit her younger sister Annie and her husband, Nick, out in Laramie while I stayed with a family friend on Cape Cod. "He studied geology when he was at

Notre Dame with Annie and Nick. Isn't that great? You know, stuff like astrobleme," she says dreamily, as if the word were a delicious bit of saltwater taffy she was chewing. "Now he's working as a geological engineer, with his own company. His latest project was an underground café." She gazes off for a long moment. "He's very strong." Then my mother grabs both of my arms and looks directly into my eyes.

"I have to tell you the most incredible thing. Angus Mathews cut off his right ear to avoid going to 'Nam."

I raise my eyebrows at my mother, and my mother smiles at me, nods.

"He went out in the backyard with a hunting knife and just sliced off his ear. Then he took an ice pick and punctured his eardrum to finish the job." My mother gives me a distracted kiss. "Isn't that heroic?"

I'm thinking it's crazy, but I don't say anything. My mother has that faraway look in her eyes—she's in love. I've seen it before, and there's nothing I can say.

At the wedding, when an older cousin asks me if I like the man my mother is going to marry, I say no.

"How could you say that?" she says, shrinking back. Then she runs to tattle. I don't honestly care.

The photographer gathers the wedding party together. My mother is dressed in an emerald green silk minidress with a rhinestone belt buckle. She is beautiful and bright-eyed, her unruly brown hair smoothed and tamed; she is smiling a brilliant white-teethed smile and gazing at Angus with obvious love and pride. Angus wears a kind of half smile—crafty. His ear looks like a mashed-up, spat-out oyster. I am in front of them. Angus has his hand on my shoulder and I am actively pulling away, my mouth open as I attempt to spin out of his grip, and out of the frame.

After the wedding in Wyoming, we drive across country to Delaware, where Angus is from and where we will now live. The cross-country trip is their honeymoon. Why I am part of this, I don't know. I'm in the backseat of the beat-up black Thunderbird, reading Native American books we bought at Chaco Canyon—each one written by a different kid from a different tribe, telling about his people, most of them vanished—while the road tears by beneath the hole in the floorboards under Angus's feet.

There is a whirlwind of Wild Turkey, piñon nuts, jokes about cowpies, more Wild Turkey. The lower the Wild Turkey gets in the bottle, which they are passing back and forth, the more I keep waiting for the fighting to begin, but so far the liquor's sloshing down around the bottom of the label and they still seem to be whooping it up. So far so good.

We stay at cheap motels along the way, Motel 6s mostly. They get me a room next to theirs, a splurge, and I just keep the TV blaring so I can't hear their activity. I learn to sleep through anything.

After some days, we arrive at Angus's parents' house. This is where the honeymoon will continue. Angus's mother's name is Maeve, and she looks just like what I'd imagined a Maeve would look like—sharp-featured, gray and veiny, with steel-colored hair pulled back in a tight bun. I'm terrified. Angus's father, whom everyone calls Boss, is abnormally tall and spruced up in a suit, with a ramrod-straight back and a militaristic twinkle in his eye. I can totally see him cracking someone over the head with a bayonet, or calmly chopping their hands off, then playing a round of golf. Years later, when I find out he was affiliated with the IRA during this time, I'm not surprised one bit.

Every morning I sit at the kitchen table eating the kind of flavored oatmeal that comes in packets. I stare uncomfortably at the closed door behind which Angus and my mother are having their honeymoon.

For a week they barely come out, except for food. There's a bathroom in the room, so they're almost self-sufficient. Music plays loudly and constantly, covering any noise they're making. Otis Redding, Wilson Pickett, and one song they play more than any other: "Slippin' Around with You," sung by Art Freeman. This song fascinates me. At the time, I think it's incredibly funky. Years later, after listening to the lyrics, I realize the song is all about cheating. In retrospect, this was an ill-conceived anthem for a honeymoon.

After the honeymoon, we rent a modest duplex in Bridgeville, Delaware. During the years I'd spent with my mother, we'd always moved pretty quickly from one house to the next. Nothing's changed with Angus Mathews.

I am learning how to read better. My father sends me a fancy gift, a three-story Dutch dollhouse from FAO Schwartz. It is my first dollhouse ever. I pose the flexible family—mother, father, daughter, son—and neatly arrange the furniture; at night I put out miniature cups of yogurt for the fairies. I still believe in fairies at this point, but the belief is tenuous. Somehow the concept of evaporation has crept in, and the empty cups with faint traces of dried yogurt the next morning are no longer proof the fairies have visited.

There is a boy in the neighborhood on whom I develop a mad crush. He has the longest eyelashes of any boy in the world. This boy is a couple of years older than me, blond, tough. Out of my league.

One day I tell him boldly, "I like you."

"What'd you say?" he says, surprised.

Before I can answer, he punches me so hard in the stomach I see stars. The wind gets knocked out of me. I double over, say nothing. I can take it.

I think, looking back, this was the first time I had a crush where I was able to knit love and pain together in a way I knew so well from my family.

It felt like home.

What I remember next is how hard this boy laughs, and how the other kids who are playing around on the lawn shout and laugh, holler and point, before they all quickly run or bike away. How my face turns bright red. How the incredible eyelashes brush against this boy's cheekbones as he studies me, disgusted.

"Don't you ever come near me again," he says under his breath, even though nobody is around anymore. "*Ever*," he hisses.

The passion in his voice, the intensity, makes me tremble; this boy has feelings for me! I think I'm going to vomit. Please don't throw up, I say silently. I'm still hunched, holding my stomach.

Then this boy tears off and cycles away down the cul-de-sac.

I remember going inside the house, the screen door snapping shut behind me. Walking, still doubled over, into my bedroom. Shutting the door. And lying curled up on the bed, replaying the moment, and the boy's face fixed on me, over and over. The soundtrack is his urgent voice: "Don't you ever come near me again."

He can't mean that. He doesn't realize it, but I know he wants the opposite. He wants me. Rachel Miranda Resnick. Six years old, and learning to read. Who wouldn't want me? He just doesn't see yet. It's my job to change it.

For a budding love junkie, this scene is a revelation. Because what happens is, the crush instantly turns into an obsession. What went wrong? How can I turn that explosion of his into passion? If he only understood how I felt, he would've embraced me as his girlfriend. I just have to try harder to impress him. That's it.

The next day I learn how to ride a bike. Fearless, focused on my shiny red two-wheeler, I pick up the skill in no time flat. I ride by the boy's house. I look for him. But the boy never speaks to me again. Still, the revelation has taken root. Even now, I sometimes think about that cruel boy with the long eyelashes and the stars he made me see.

In our next house in Bridgeville, a one-story ranch on Polk Road, I play with Matchbox cars and a Betty Crocker oven, in addition to the beloved dollhouse.

Now the fighting begins. I can hear them yelling as they come in at night, after barhopping. My mother's always been a beer drinker, or alternated with cheap red Chianti in the basket. Angus, though, favors Jack Daniel's. I've seen the bottles in the garbage.

"Who is he?" screams Angus Mathews. "Just tell me who he is."

Sometimes my mother shouts back, sometimes she bursts into tears. I want to comfort her, but I am afraid of Angus Mathews and his mangled ear.

Instead, I take even more care in ordering my dollhouse. Everything has to be just so. I am meticulous with cleaning, arranging the furniture, placing the miniature plates of painted wood food, grooming the dolls. They are perfect.

My mother is pregnant.

One morning Angus offers to drive me to school. Panicked, I try to catch my mother's eye, but she is delighted he's taking an interest.

We get in his black Thunderbird. I can barely close the door, it's so heavy. When Angus shuts his door with a tremendous thud, it rocks the whole car. Angus doesn't speak to me until we are on the main street. Then he slows way down, as if to pull off the side of the road.

"Who is he?"

I take my time answering, speak in a very small voice, making myself tiny, perhaps invisible if I try hard enough.

"I don't understand," I say.

He leaves one hand on the steering wheel, puts his other hand on the seat right near me, and leans in, his ragged ear so close I can see the white score marks around what's left of the shredded lobe, and whispers, "Who is your mother seeing? What's his name?"

I clutch the armrest until my knucklebones pop white under my skin, say nothing, just count, count billboards, Stop signs, IHOP, out-of-state license plates, count all the way until we get to the school.

One night, Angus Mathews punches my mother in the face. A beer bottle breaks. I watch the scene unfold in the living room through the open door of my bedroom, from my bunk bed, still as a corpse, unable to suss out an escape route, hoping they'll forget about me.

"I'm going to get my shotgun, and then I'm going to come back and shoot you both, goddammit!" says Angus. Then he slams out of the house, peels out of the driveway.

My mother's face is swollen, already purpling and raw.

That night, we take off—she many months pregnant, me clutching my security blanket Pink and the cat in my arms—before he returns. Good-bye, Polk Road. We flee to New York, and with the help of some of my mother's friends, we find a rental and take up residence in Alphabet City.

In our new shabby apartment, shortly after we arrive in New York, my mother challenges me to take a good picture of her black eye for the court case; if I do, I'll get to keep the Polaroid camera. I do.

That night, I remember desperately wanting the cat Chocolate Chip to cuddle with me, to purr, to just stay put, to be mine.

I tie blue hair yarn around his neck and tie the other end to the post of the upper bunk bed, where I sleep. He immediately leaps off the top bunk and almost strangles himself. I can still feel his claws bite sharply into my skin, can still see his cat eyes rolling wildly, staring at me with hatred and fear. I have never told anyone this secret before now.

Back on Polk Road, Angus takes an ax and chops up the rocking chair from West 110th Street where my mother used to rock me and weep over her first husband. Then Angus Mathews takes the ax and hacks my dollhouse to pieces.

Maybe it was the animals that spoke so intimately to my mother, or nature itself, which she loved so passionately, but the year before she died, she turned to religion. St. Francis of Assisi in particular. In those final months, she took to sending me cards filled with St. Francis of Assisi's teachings and prayers. One of the last ones she ever mailed included these words: "Lord, grant that I might not so much seek to be loved as to love."

I wonder whether, toward the end, my mother was trying to figure out her lifelong struggles with men and relationships. Although I had little contact with her during this period, friends of hers told me that she had stopped drinking, that she was going to meetings for recovering alcoholics. They told me she was intensely focused on getting her two children back in her custody. I like to imagine that my mother found comfort in those words of St. Francis of Assisi, and that maybe she glimpsed another way one could experience love before she died, but I will never know.

I do know those words continue to haunt me, and to inspire deeper reflection as I turn now to the men in my life.

CHAPTER THREE

Euphoria: Agony and Ecstasy

2006

When my lover Winchester was three years old, his father spat in his mouth; that's how he let his son know he was too old to kiss him anymore.

I want to know why I am drawn almost exclusively to men who have been emotionally damaged and whom, in turn, I allow in various ways to emotionally damage me. Why do I choose these men again and again—confusing sex with love, confusing emotional pain with more love—and take rejection as an invitation to come back asking, sometimes begging, for more.

Does emotional agony somehow heighten the sex? And why does my twisted mind translate that agony as "true love"?

Am I, in fact, addicted to something powerfully destructive I get from these men?

Addiction is defined as the inability to resist a habit, an uncontrollable compulsion to repeat a behavior regardless of the consequences.

I'm an addict.

More than anything, I want to know how I can transcend this; how I can fill the void I look for these men to fill; how I can become whole, become well-loved, and learn to love well in return.

Fun, huh?

The prospect of facing this mortifying track record makes me cringe, so let me tell you next about a man who at least didn't lie to me from the start. He didn't, like many of the others, pretend to be a mensch, or a man in search of a wife. His name is Winchester Grandview Harrington. He's not the first, but our painful relationship is exemplary of the bad choices I made. Also, I think he will be easier to confront than some of the others.

I was thirty-eight, and I thought I was looking for a life partner. I wanted a child. I imagined myself raising a daughter, traveling with her, giving her the sense of adventure and passion for art and culture that my mother had given me, but getting right all the things my parents had gotten wrong: I would spend time with her, set boundaries, be stable. I would never ever abandon her.

But instead, I did the same damn thing I usually did. I chose a sex god. He was drop-dead gorgeous. I handed him my heart and asked again and again for the love he wasn't capable of giving.

"Hey brother," says the doorman, slapping Winchester's hand at the entrance to the club, giving me the once-over. "Haven't seen you in a few weeks."

Instantly jealous, I wonder if Winchester comes here with other women.

"Five bucks," says the doorman.

Winchester hesitates. "Five bucks!" he says, striking a bug-eyed mock-shocked pose.

Without thinking, I fumble through my shoulder bag. "Here, let me," I say quickly, offering my open wallet. There isn't much in it. Winchester takes a five, and pulls out a five from his jeans' pocket. The doorman doesn't blink. This going-dutch move could mean Winchester is a modern man, casual, and I shouldn't expect to be paid for.

Or maybe that's how they do it in Tortola. My brain is a minefield, erupting random theories.

Blowin' Smoke and the Smokettes rip into funky old-school blues, filling the small, sexy dark room that is Harvelle's. The place is jammed, the patrons buzzing to the nine-piece band. Bodies dip and sway, lipstick glistens. It's as close to a juke joint as you'll get in white-bread Santa Monica, drawing people from across the sprawling city: all ages, all ethnicities, some slumming, some stepping out—like us.

Winchester is way better-looking than I am. However, because I'm blonde (thanks to expensive highlights) and voluptuous (read: big-breasted and thick-waisted), if I dress in cleavage-revealing, leg-baring clothes and turn up the volume on my personality, I can bring it. Tonight I do. I imagine radiator waves of heat lifting off our bodies, generated by our chemistry, our visual impact. Winchester is stunning—six foot two, ebony-skinned, hard-bodied, full-lipped, and fine, with showy short dreads and glam hip-hop style. He's country church-boy with a touch of femme and a soulful vulnerability in his eyes. Even though I'm no actor, going out in public with a man I'm hot for, who's hot for me, feels like theater. And I am an exhibitionist. All eyes on me, I feel loved, desired, relished. Seen.

Winchester leads us right to the middle of the dance floor. We both need this—to be the center of attention.

Though I don't realize it then, I'm tamping down the insecurity that comes from being with a man who's prettier. I have always had a weakness for lookers and have sought them out. I will brazenly approach these men. My friend Stasia calls it "shiny penny syndrome." If a guy has flash, if he telegraphs danger, if he's cocky, good-looking, if he dresses better than me, whether gangster or prince, if he's broadcasting universal sex appeal—I'm there. Much later I understand this attraction has something to do with not only how inadequate I think I look, but also how monstrously ugly I feel deep down inside.

"Win-ches-ter!" shouts a spastic older guy with a skinny tie as he comes running up to us. "I've been practicing your dance moves. Look!" And he contorts his body as if he's having an epileptic seizure, tries to spin, and ends up getting his shoe caught on the beer-stained floorboards. We politely clap for him and then turn our attention to each other.

"I'm not that good a dancer," I say softly. "I've never even taken a dance class."

"Just follow me," Winchester says. "Let me lead you."

He pulls me to him, clasps me against his chest. While his hips gyrate, his strong thighs press against mine, cuing me when to shift my feet to the pounding rhythm. Meanwhile, this guy stays right with us, circling, grinning, watching Winchester's moves, winking at me. He's not the only one. A little solar system is forming around my partner. People are waving, pointing Winchester out on the dance floor. Women are actually licking their lips, bending their bodies toward him.

Winchester spins me out and around; I am dizzy. I imagine walking to the bathroom and Winchester following, hoisting me up on the sink, taking me right there. As if he's reading my mind, Winchester whispers, "I've had sex on the dance floor."

I stare. You would think I'd be put off, but no. I'm in thrall.

"Go on," I say, encouraging him to tell me more. Because this is one dance, the sexual dance, the love dance, I understand. This is one dance class I don't need to take.

"It's dark. We're in a corner of the club. The dance floor's packed. I hold the girl from behind, hold her hips, slide her dress up . . . we keep dancing." He brushes a strand of hair back from my face. "I've done this a few times. In Paris, Tokyo. In Trellis Bay."

"L.A.?" I say. Egging him on. Wanting nothing more than to be the next dance-fuck notch. Then blushing with jealousy about the other women who've been there before, wanting no part of it, ashamed. Then once again, uncontrollably, burning with excitement from the newly implanted fantasy. It's as if I can already feel the pulse of him against me, rocking my hips to the beat as people watch.

This is our seventh meeting. My mind, my heart, are running in the worn groove of an old, old pattern. Sex is obsession. Obsession is love. It follows that I'm ready to have his child. I met Winchester poolside at the Standard Hotel two weeks before we slept together on our fourth meeting, after dancing in my living room to Patsy Cline.

"Come to me, Mama. Come to me COD," croons the lead singer, sweat pouring from his brow, sweat tracing a lazy line down his bare chest. Red from the glowing neon wall sign radiates out, fuses with the spinning disco ball overhead. It catches and spills polka dots of silvery-red light over the vibrating crowd.

My fantasy inflames. Till death do us part, we exchange vows in a pool of disco light.

An ex-ballet dancer, trained in complicated lifts and the art of leverage, Winchester raises me in the air. Time stops. The trumpet notes hold, shimmer, glide along with the husky Smokettes' raw yet honeyed syllables. I'm a big-boned woman, muscled. No one's lifted me in the air since I was a child.

When the music ends, everyone clears to the side of the dance floor. Everyone except us. We don't care, keep grinding against each other, Winchester graceful and fluid, tall and striking with his doe eyes and dreads, holding me close, swaying me into his hips, me in my skintight black dress and spiky high heels, trying to follow his moves.

Just then, in one of those hot-weather power outages from all the air-conditioning, the lights go out. The whole place turns pitch-black. And still, we keep dancing—slow dancing. You could say this was romantic. You could also say this was high-octane mutual obsession. This, now, is better than sex. Sex will come later. I know this. Everybody in Harvelle's knows this. Knowing they know turns me on.

Within ten minutes someone's found the fuse box and turned the lights back on.

When we leave, the doorman grins. "You two were so red hot on the dance floor, I believe you put those lights out."

And I'm proud when he says this. Like I've made an impact. I've made a mark. When I'm in the arms of a man, I forget there's any other satisfaction in life.

A coyote slinks rapidly across the road, eyes flaring red in the headlights' glare, disappears. I'm taking the tight S curves fast, whipping past dense foliage and soaring canyon mountains on either side, my foot heavy on the pedal. Winchester's right on my tail, gunning his baby blue Mustang with the creamy white top. I cut right at the feed store, tear up Entrada. The curves are so tight up here on the narrow one-lane road I think I've lost him. It's mostly dark, except for a few scattered porch lamps.

I crest the steep rise of Observation, stop short, wait. My pulse pounds with lust. I don't breathe until the two beams from Winchester's Mustang come into sight.

When we park and kill the engines, there is only the sound of them ticking down into silence. And the chirr-croak of the tree frogs. And us breathing as we hustle to my door, Winchester behind, close, hands hot on my body, propelling me. We stop for a moment to look at the night sky, see the bright stars popping through, listen to the low haunting call of a hoot owl.

Inside, I put Lima, the spoiled four-year-old mini-macaw, to bed.

"Don't freak out," I say, draping his sheets and blankets over the cage. "I know there's a man here, but you're way better-looking."

The bird makes his sleep-time throat purr.

In a few weeks, my beloved Lima will get snatched off the deck by a bobcat. Months of mourning and depression will follow. Then I will rescue the scarlet macaw Ajax as a tribute to Lima, but nothing will take away the pain of this loss.

"Good night," I sing-song softly, embarrassed but also hoping Winchester can still hear. "I love you." I put my index finger through the cage in our nightly ritual, and Lima nips it lightly.

Then we're inside the bedroom, and this man—who earlier tonight at Harvelle's hoisted me up in the air, spun me to the sultry blues beat, dipped and led me—picks me up and throws me down on the bed. I don't even have to tell him this is how I like it. He seems to know. It's as if we really did meet up those many years ago in Bridgeville, Delaware, where, strangely, we later discover, we both briefly lived. Maybe he was the boy with the long-lashed eyes who punched me so hard I saw stars, even though that boy was blond and white and mean, and I've been waiting years since Eddie Vaughan, my last big love, to feel that punch again, that deep-down flutter in the heart of hearts.

I lie here so excited I'm paralyzed. This man is a god. Even the air gets wavy around him.

I didn't tell you the whole story when I presented him as an ex–ballet dancer. He was that. He was also an exotic dancer, who had a rabid fan base in Tokyo; he was also an underwear model. Are you with me?

At the time, I thought this was as good as it got—I thought this was the greatest thing a man could offer me. Friendship? Inconceivable. Marriage? Pure fantasy. But an underwear model who wouldn't love me back? This was—oh, this was pure bliss. Never mind the painful yearning, the sleepless nights that followed his frequent disappearances. Forget about the tears I shed when he blew me off. When he did show up, all that anguish only fed the flame. This had to be love.

Ladies and gentlemen, Winchester Grandview Harrington is taking off his clothes.

He tugs off his biker boots and sets them neatly next to the desk, toes pointing toward the window. He twists his torso, unbuckles his brown leather belt, pulls it through the loops, and drapes it over the chair. Then he slides his ripped jeans down over his white jockeys and folds the jeans neatly. An underwear model in his underwear. Even the slight bow in his legs only adds to the vision, lending what the Japanese call *wabi-sabi*, the imperfection that makes true perfection.

Pantherlike, he pounces on the bed, on my body, manhandles me into a fierce headlock while I try to hold my own.

"Gotcha," he says. Please fuck me, I want to say, but I don't have to say it; he knows. Which doesn't mean it'll happen right now. Luckily I love grappling. Wrestling. Rolling around. The feel of him subduing me with one expert hold after another. He is like the older brother I never had. He is family. Unfortunately I'm only an expert in one kind of family.

"I can take you," I say, slipping out of his grip by using every ounce of energy I have, then squeezing his legs as hard as I can and bear-hugging him around the chest.

"Girl, I'll make you choke on those words," Winchester says, as with one fluid move he flips me on my back and starts tickling my ribs. After a few minutes, I'm breathless. He has me trapped. I want to relax into his body, his grip, but I'm still feigning struggle. Then I give up, exhausted. I let him envelop me. He wins. Minutes tick; my desire grows. He refuses to touch me sexually until I'm insane with need.

When he finally kisses my neck, I almost have a stroke.

"Take your shoes off," he says. I do. "Now your dress."

I sweep the thin black material over my head, toss it on the floor.

"Let me see you. Keep these on."

He slowly traces my breasts, sends psychedelic currents through my nervous system. Then he pulls the plastic coil bracelet from his wrist and binds up his crazy spring-sronging hair, scoots down my body, sliding the silk thong underwear aside as he goes . . .

Not only is the sex mind-blowing, cataclysmic, and ecstatic, it's deliciously unsustainable over time. Nirvana touched—then torn away. Because as giving and godlike as he is during sex, he is equally withholding in every other way.

For me, Winchester is like pure heroin.

When the second Magnum condom breaks, Winchester doesn't get another.

We are one. Meant to be. This much is clear. How could it be anything else? I told him last week if I got pregnant, I would have the child. Even if I had to raise it alone. He knows this. I am secretly exultant. If he's having unprotected sex with me, he must love me. Right? How could he not love me forever, after sex that spectacular? I can see our child, bouncing between us, Winchester kissing her sweetly, lifting her up in the air so the child laughs delightedly; I can see Winchester and me still clubbing when we're sixty, the other patrons clearing a path for us as we hit the dance floor . . .

After sex, he pulls away from me, rolls toward the wall. I frown in the dark. Why won't he spoon me, after what we just shared? After practically signing a love contract to father my child?

"Whatcha thinking?" I say lamely.

"Nunya."

"Huh?"

"Nunya business! That's what we say in Tortola." He chuckles, and I move in closer. I lay my hands on his shoulders, stroke them gently, erotically. I'm ready to go again. This ability of mine to go and go, this insatiable need for sex, is one of the bonds I create in relationships. I forge a chain playfully disguised as a ribbon—a masquerade of natural abandon and innocent lust. So of course I think he will be pleased. Turned on.

Instead, he shakes me from his back. "Your hands are so heavy."

My face burns in the dark. I have always been ashamed of my hands.

My hands are wrinkled and lined, leathery dry, as they've been since I was a young child. Even adults would grab them and say, "What's wrong with your hands?"

"Monkey hands, monkey hands," the children would chant in the schoolyard, on the bus.

When I told my mother, she took my hands in hers, studied them carefully. "You've got old soul hands."

I tried to snatch them back. I shouldn't have asked her. She was drunk. As usual, she fixed her pale blue eyes on me with hypnotic intensity.

"You've been across the river Styx and come back," she said, staring deep into my eyes. "You are my special daughter."

She took another slug of beer. I pretended I had to go the bathroom and ran upstairs and locked myself in my room. I knew what was across the river Styx. The Land of the Dead. The three-headed dog that guarded the gates of hell. I dropped Gloria Gaynor's 45 "Don't Leave Me This Way" on the record player and cranked the volume so loud I wouldn't hear if my mother knocked on the door. Then I put on the homemade sunglasses I'd fashioned out of wire, with blue cellophane glued on for lenses, sat on the lower bunk, and sang along.

In bed with Winchester, our skin not touching anywhere, I suddenly remember who else had heavy hands.

Though Winchester has barely spoken of his mother in the short time we've known each other, I do know that she illegally smuggled Tortolans into the States for a steep price, that she's a fearsome churchgoing woman with an all-consuming greed for money who used to dress up her pretty boys in flashy Sunday suits, who hit, pelted, kicked, and stomped "sense" into the boys while their father gardened and stayed out of the house and away from her until he finally left.

I look at my hands in horror. There's no denying they are manly and gnarled. How could I ever think these hands would wear a ring given by a man? That these hands would ever inspire someone to commit? And somehow this moment of self-abasement gets tangled up with the heightened desire, the sexual energy, and it's all very familiar. This is what I do, what I feel. We find each other—the damaged ones, our energies prickling in recognition even before we meet. Across crowded rooms at Hollywood parties, wandering grocery aisles, blading on Venice Beach. Anywhere. Everywhere. Instantly. We always have our love lights turned on, seeking willing partners. I can smell their lust for domination, sense the pleasure they draw from crushing. They in turn can see the capacity for hurt beneath my bold come-hither gaze. When the first psychic blow falls, then, and only then, I am hooked. I know. Because it's what I've been doing and feeling and craving for years.

I slowly move away from Winchester, toward my side of the bed. There I fold my arms around myself, keep my body rigid at the edge of the mattress. Not that it matters. Winchester doesn't notice. Instead, I am plagued by the intense desire to touch him. I don't fall asleep for hours. Even his breathing is sultry. I'm so gone for him.

Lima wakes us in the morning by banging plastic toys against the bars. "Hello? . . ."

There is Winchester, his head burrowed into the pillow, his leg thrown over mine. I want to cement last night, this moment, seal this man to me. All's well with the sun streaming in, the bird squawking for breakfast. It's a new day; my lover, future husband, father of my child, is here by my side. Just then Winchester reaches out and pulls me into a tight embrace.

"I woke up thinking about that night I met you," I say shyly.

He's got me tight in his arms. I breathe my words against his shoulder, the soft skin. "How good you looked, sexier than anyone—I had to meet you."

Winchester pushes me away from him and stares at me directly. "I wasn't attracted to you at all," he says.

Lima picks up a water bottle from the bottom of the cage and throws it against the bars with his beak. The plasticky crash makes Winchester wince. A wave of desperation shudders through me. I tear up.

"My philosophy is complete honesty," he says.

And then, to my shock, he nuzzles my neck, plants feathery kisses around my earlobe.

And I let him do it.

Last night he was too cheap to pay my dance-club admission. He had sex with me, then insulted my hands, my looks. Now he's leveraging my hips against his own.

I let him do this too.

Lima loses patience. "Hello! Hello! HELLO! Good morning. Step up. Step up. STEP UP!"

I won't lose patience for another year.

I understand all this quite clearly.

Which doesn't matter at all. Understanding doesn't help; I am unable to stop. The adrenaline rush, the savagery—I confess that it all feels good, like lashes from a superbly oiled whip. The sting penetrates to my deepest chambers. Not only does the pain wake me, tingling every nerve, but it also feels like destiny. It feels like coming home.

Where did I even learn this cruel dance?

*   *   *

Breakfast at the Big House this morning is wild blueberries, pancakes, and beer. That's what Ma's drinking. So's the babysitter, Tyler, a really cute guy who just graduated college and has blond hair that flops over his eyes. Why can't he be my boyfriend? Tyler and my mom are whispering, their beer bottles clattering against the Formica table when they set them down.

We are in the kitchen, which is cramped, even though the family's summer Cape Cod house is huge. My grandparents, her parents, are at either end of the kitchen table, drinking martinis. The sound of the martini shaker is the sound of summer. This starts at eight A.M. every day. Aunt Totty is resplendent in tennis whites. My mother wears a dashiki over her bathing suit. She thinks she's fat, and she kind of is.

"You look like Phyllis Diller," she says, pointing at my rat's-nest hair.

"You look like Medusa," I say. Too bad she gave me the D'Aulaires' Greek mythology books, 'cuz now I know stuff. My hair might be snarled, but hers is snaky with reddish-brown curls.

"I have a WASP-Afro, daughter. Clearly one of our hallowed British ancestors slept with a black man," she says to her mother, who has big, raised blue-green veins in her legs and wears orthopedic shoes and wraparound skirts with appliquéd pictures of horses, dogs, and hunters. "But no one will tell. Right, Mum?"

"Why is everyone drinking in the morning?" I ask, pouring more syrup on my pancakes and grabbing a fistful of blueberries from the colander. I am seven years old.

My mother laughs her maniacal laugh, pinches Tyler on the cheek. No one answers me. My grandfather, Doctor Fitzgerald, looks like a classic movie star, except he has red veins that spray all over his nose and across his face. Gin blossoms, my mother says. But they don't look like flowers to me.

"WHY IS EVERYONE DRINKING IN THE MORNING?" I say.

Grannie speaks over my head to her favorite daughter, Aunt Totty, short for Tottleworth. I think she's Grannie's favorite because she is thin.

"Isn't summer lovely?" she says. "Just super."

Later that morning, my cousin Bobby and I are on the third floor, where all us kids sleep, and no one else is around. "Come here," he whispers, leading me into the back dormer room for the boy cousins. I have my own room because there are fewer girl cousins.

In the back of that room, there's a small latched door. Bobby creaks it open. I squat down, then crawl in. Bobby follows me, then closes the door.

"Shhh," he whispers, flicking on a flashlight. We have to crouch, it's so small. There are wooden beams and slats pressing down on us, and tons of cobwebs. Way in the corner of the tiny space someone shoved some dusty boxes that look like they're disintegrating.

"Lift up your dress," he says.

Bobby is awesomely mean. He's a year older. Whenever he passes me on the stairs to the third floor, he whispers things like "wretch" under his breath. The nasty word creeps in like

I imagine an earwig would, staining everything with an indelible ink that blooms darkly inside my body and fills me with hot shame. It's horrible and strangely thrilling at the same time.

Bobby had authority over me back then—maybe because nobody else wanted it. When Bobby ordered me around, he instinctively understood that I was craving someone, anyone, to tell me what to do. No matter what it was.

"Pull down your underwear."

I do. Bobby leans in closer, trains the flashlight beam right there.

"Okay. Let's go," he says.

"I want to see too," I say, stubborn.

Scowling, he yanks down his swim trunks. A bunch of sand scatters on the floor. There, in between his legs, dangles what looks like a cross between a toadstool and a slimy clam foot, pebble smooth and weird. Blood rushes to my face and I feel really queasy.

"Let's go," he says, hiking up his swim trunks and pushing me out the door. Bobby runs downstairs.

We don't tell anyone.

But all afternoon, the secret burns in me. I'm afraid that someone will find out, that I will be punished. The burning sensation makes me feel both sick and pleased. I can't stop thinking about what happened.

Alone in my bedroom, which looks out over the bay, I sit Indian style, catch a slow-moving daddy longlegs by one leg. That leg now hangs useless. I pull it off. Count. There are seven more. I pull another. Six. The daddy longlegs topples, skitters. I catch it again. Pull another leg. Another. Until it is only a speck on the gray-painted floorboards.

Very late that same night, Bobby appears at my bed.

"Wake up, wretch. Time to dig to China."

"China?" I say, sitting up in bed, still hot from sleep. Bobby sits next to me, lightly slaps my cheek.

"Get up."

We go down the third-floor stairs, slip along the long back hallway, tiptoe down another set of stairs to the first floor, unlatch the door, and pad out onto the lawn. The dewy grass feels spongy under my feet. I step on a piece of moss that feels like silk. Then we're on a narrow beach path. Sand and sea grass. I'm afraid to step on a pricker.

Then Bobby turns on his flashlight, shines it in my face. We're standing in the sand.

Bobby is tall, his arms ropy and muscled from swimming and pounding his younger brother, Lucas. At least he hasn't hit me, but he could. He's not the kind of cousin you want to mess with. I'm cold. The beach doesn't look any fun at night—all shadows and odd whistling, scraping noises. Even the ocean sounds ominous, slapping at the shore. I imagine a bunch of horseshoe crabs scuttling along the seaweed, dragging their spiny tails. Sand fleas jump around, bite my ankles. I breathe in the thick salty air, wait quietly to be told what to do. Not even Tyler, who's supposed to be the babysitter, tells me what to do.

"Dig," Bobby says.

"How?"

"Use your hands," he says with disdain.

I bend down and dig with my hands. The more I dig, the more the sand spills back into the hole. That won't stop me. I'm grateful to be singled out. To be chosen. He likes me, is what I think. Boys are just weird. I'm pleased I'm figuring things out. A secret thrill sparks through me. Maybe it's the attention. Maybe it's the closeness. Maybe it's the relief of not being alone. So I keep digging. For a long time.

Until my cousin says to stop.

The day after Winchester and I slept together for the first time, I sat at the computer, my restless fingers poised on the keys.

All day I had replayed sensory images—a flash of thigh, the feel of his hand on my hips, an animal utterance, a brush of his lips against my neck. They crowded my mind. Short-circuited my brain. I could think of nothing else.

I struggled not to write to Winchester. I did what I did when I was anxious. When I needed distraction: I sprang Lima from his cage.

He strutted along the top of the open cage door, raised his iridescent green wings in greeting, stared at me expectantly.

"Peanut?" I said to Lima, handing him his favorite treat.

The bird's eyes flared with excitement. He cracked the shell with his beak, then, divalike, flung the shell on the floor. When I walked into the bedroom/office, he slid down the cage-door bars like a tiny feathered fireman and chased after me. I returned to the computer, sat before it in a trance. Lima tugged at my pants with his beak, wanting to play.

"Let the man contact you," I said. "Right, Lima?"

The bird climbed on my shoulder, pressed his soft featherless bird face against my cheek in a gesture of affection. This filled me with a rush of longing.

I began to type. "Dear Winchester." I erased that, wrote, "Hey W." Better. More casual.

But then I typed a line from a poem I admire.

"Every time you wish the sky was something happening to your heart, you lose twice."

Don't write too long, my brain chattered. Wrap it up. I did.

"Now you have my first e-mail. Short, but studded with a line that acts like a stone thrown in water to me, causing ripples that keep on coming."

It was only two paragraphs long. A record of brevity for me. I hit Send. Then panicked. Reread. Clever double entendre. Reread. Stupid double entendre! Reread again. Savored Olena Kalytiak Davis's line of poetry. Fought the urge to send another e-mail. Broke down. And wrote one more. This time I wrote for pages. Then, in a superhuman feat of restraint, I didn't hit Send. Instead, I saved it in my private ongoing cyberjournal.

Hours later, way past his bedtime, Lima was still on my shoulder. He was making that clicking sound birds make at night. It is the equivalent of human snoring.

Here's what happened. It makes me sick to tell it. Winchester and I would have sex. He would go home. I'd be flying high all morning. In the afternoon it would start wearing off. Around teatime, when low blood sugar would hit, I'd panic he didn't feel the same way. I'd brew a cup of espresso. Then I'd sit down at the computer and write to him. Words, paragraphs, pages, more pages. Bad poetry. E-mails full of yearning. Each one I sent as a kind of mental tattoo. Don't forget! Here's your souvenir from Rachelville!

Because I already knew, as my mother had taught me early and well, that men leave.

For these first months, I try to keep things light, sexy. And when I'm writing those e-mails, I actually think I'm doing just that. Like, with lines like this:

"Your body's imprinted on mine, and chemistry enough to prompt canaries and even scrub jays to sing arias and give birth to baby neurons all at once."

If I need to write more, I try to save it for my journal. Still, the e-mails I do send are lengthy and dense. I try to pretend they're not invested with feeling, not overwrought with the desire to impress. Problem is, I can't help myself from e-mailing him.

Winchester writes back. But not as often. And not as long.

And like any sane person receiving such an emotion-drenched barrage, he warns me off. One day he writes he "won't look too far down whatever road," prompting a flurry of impassioned replies from me.

A few days later, he points out, accurately, that there's "a weighted quality to the way you express yourself."

"I can't tell you all the times I have imagined calling and asking you to come over in the middle of the night, no talk no questions." I write.

"My whole body misses you, like another creature," I write.

Weighted? With bottomless desire focused on him? No kidding.

"I wish I could be your angel, make you see," he writes,

trying once again to gently rebuff. I, however, sense an opening. An easing. A chance.

Now I know just how to respond. I quote Kafka's words about how "a book must be the ax for the frozen sea within us," then go on to gush:

"Well, my sea ain't frozen. You hacked it up but good. Left me liquefied. Liquidated. My insides molten, lava-tranced. The sea, the sea. That's me. I love that image of a man spreading over his lover like liquid."

I go on and on.

This e-mail is the tipping point, because one morning Winchester wakes up and silences me with a warning finger. "Don't say it—I see poetry coming in your eyes."

Then he tells me point-blank, "You're wasting emotion on me. I don't believe in love."

This is the kind of love I recognize. The one where the conflicted lover pretends he doesn't feel the way he does feel, must feel. We are still having sex. Unprotected. I'm not pregnant. Winchester no longer stays in the morning. There are no more days spent in bed, no more breakfasts together after passionate nights. He leaves earlier and earlier. Then he gets busy on Saturday nights. Weekends. When we do see each other, he often comes by late. Forget dinner. Forget dancing. I don't try to cuddle anymore. I have learned my lesson. I have turned thirty-nine.

One morning, Winchester's tone is accusing. I have overstepped. He tells me, again, he is not available, is not looking for a relationship, and then says bluntly, "I know what you're looking for. We're not on the same page."

This pattern with Winchester repeats over and over with increasing harshness. I get more frantic. I can't believe Winchester hasn't fallen for me. I can't believe I haven't gotten pregnant. I can't believe I'm heading, hurtling, toward forty. I am out of my mind.

Every time he leaves after a night of sex—at my place, never his—I fire off a volley of après-sex missives. Especially if he's unexpectedly taken me out dancing, like in the beginning, and given me hope.

"Dancing was way fun, intoxicating, as was the after-dancing," I write. "I'm deliciously sex-drunk and sore and sated (also newly insatiable)."

This one goes on for pages of desperation-fueled semi-erotic nonsense.

He writes back. Indeed, he sends a poem. My hopes soar. I knew it! Keep at it. Don't give up. Stay steady. Show your fidelity. And he'll come around. He'll open up. He'll trust in the relationship. Declarations of love can't be far off, can they?

"I want to print your poem out and . . . pretend you're here, groove on the thought, the feel of you, the tastes of your words, the sound of your sibilance, something like that."

Winchester responds by not calling.

I send a flurry of impassioned e-mail.

Winchester says, "You're pushing, Rachel."

I send an über-clever e-mail: "This Is Not a Valentine . . . and you are not an object of my desire, nor a muse to my heart and mind . . . on this Thursday, February 14th, I will not crush and press the petals of a thousand roses into service of perfuming the contents of this note that is not a valentine, addressed to you who do not stir me . . ." and so on, for a full ten pages, ending with "all I know is when we touch, something burns through."

Winchester forgets it's my birthday and misses my party.

I send a lengthy accusing e-mail.

Winchester replies, "You're doing that thing again. Taking this too seriously."

I do have a shred of self-awareness at this point. For example, I'm aware that I know how to do this. I know exactly how to do this. Don't I have a father who gave then withdrew, gave then withdrew? Not to mention the other family members. I can handle the push-pull. I will pretend to back off, give him room to breathe, so he can come to his senses on his own.

I write him another long e-mail ending with this: "The jasmine is in full bloom on the deck and smells like heaven. There is a tree below the deck which is also in full blossom, white-flowered, and it looks like cherry blossoms. Stunning. Wish I could share it with you. Ciao, Rachel."

I don't fool him with that "ciao."

He writes back: "I am not in love with you."

I walk out onto the deck, breathe, gather up all my dignity.

Then I sit down at my computer.

The man I've been sleeping with for nine months has just said he's not in love with me. But I've been here before. I know precisely what to do. I write him another long, vein-sluicing response.

That dog don't hunt. This girl don't quit. Utter insanity. I continue to write. I ask him more questions, hoping they will make him see things differently. I browbeat, I retreat, I cajole, I seduce.

Winchester—who fits perfectly, chemically, into my crazy need—writes back just enough to keep me going. And periodically, of course, he comes over for mind-blowing sex.

Winchester is like pure heroin. But that's only because I am an addict.

We are in the living room in my parents' old apartment on West 110th Street in Manhattan, my father and I, dancing to the record player. Maybe I'm three. It's a rare occasion, my father in the apartment and us doing something together. Even when he was there, he didn't like to play with me that much. Mostly he was gone. On trips. To California. He would come back with yoga books and bottles of vitamins. The fighting between him and Ma would start right away though, and he would leave again.

"Splish splash I was taking a bath . . ."

My father slips and slides in his wool socks, holding my hands as I dance my bare feet along the dusty wood floor. I'm looking up at him. He's tall and dark-haired way up there near the ceiling. I'm trying to keep up, anything to make it last.

He sings along. After a while he makes a *blub-blub-blub* sound and spins me around.

Laughter gurgles up through my body. Out of the corner of my eye I see the record needle moving across the 45, it's almost over, so I wave my hands wildly in the air, jump my feet around in a silly zigzag. The record hisses to a stop.

"Daddy! More, more, more!"

I tug at my father's hand. That doesn't work either. He frees his hand. Our dance was just a moment's distraction for him.

He's headed for the yoga mat, where he will stand on his head for a whole half hour, ignoring me, and then he will read the *New York Times* for hours. I will pull at his baggy pants. I will try to grab his glasses. I will somersault in front of him. No matter what I do, he will stay glued to the paper.

The next year, when I'm four, my father moves out. I turn five in 1968 and fall in love with Ringo Starr. In my dreams, he will not leave me because he's so grateful someone chose him, not Paul. We live happily ever after upside down on the ceiling, eating Cap'n Crunch cereal that never gets soggy and pulling rainbows from our hair. There are no cockroaches allowed in the land where Ringo and I live.

Every birthday after my father moves out, before blowing out the candles on my cake, I secretly wish that my father would leave his new wife and he and my mother would get back together. The concentration required for this wish is world-class. Olympian. Usually I prepare days in advance of my birthday, focusing my attention on building houses of cards, timing myself on how fast I can put together puzzles. If I can only say it convincingly enough, if I mean it enough, if every bit of energy I have is poured into this one chant, then, for sure, it'll happen. I only quit repeating this wish when I am eight years old. The same year I finally stop sucking my thumb. When my father and his wife have two children, out of four to come, it gets impossible to imagine him ever coming home to me and my mother.

I've got the midnight disease bad, what they call hyper-graphia—the compulsion to write. I steamroll right over

Winchester's warnings: "I can't get hooked," he says once. "I think you give me too much," he says, delicately, another time.

Finally, he writes that he no longer wants to have sex. Let's just be friends.

This prompts a bombardment of e-mails from Rachelville.

And then he checks out completely. "I don't want to be held hostage by your feelings for me," he writes, in what had to be a huge burst of mental health.

This note stops me cold. But not for long. I write again, just checking in.

He writes back . . . from New York. Sanely, he's moved three thousand miles away.

After my father moves out, I visit him occasionally.

I am five years old.

He remarried only six weeks after he and my mother divorced. His new wife is named Batsheva. This name takes me a while to pronounce right. I know she is German Jewish, from Washington Heights. And a pediatrician. But I haven't yet met her.

Whenever I arrive, Batsheva is gone.

Their apartment is filled with modern furniture—a purple modular couch, a glass-top dining table with shiny chrome legs. The gray carpet is new, or vacuumed so carefully it looks that way. I can't find a dust bunny anywhere. I am afraid to touch anything for fear of leaving a fingerprint. I am afraid to sit anywhere in case I dent the stuffing, or tear a thread in the upholstery. Surfaces gleam in warning. Even the black lacquered coffee table is sharp to the touch.

Today, my father teaches me how to play paddleball. You hold this wooden racket with a red rubber ball stapled to a long rubber band, and you hit it over and over. I can't do it more than three times, but my father can do it a hundred times.

"I was the champion at summer camp," he says. "Nobody could beat me." Then he tells me a secret. "The food wasn't good, but the cherry pie was delicious. So after everyone went to sleep, I snuck back in the cafeteria . . . and I ate all the cherry pie."

My father is talented. And funny. And a little mischievous.

When it's time to take a bath, I am excited. This tub is deeper than my mother's tub. The water is hot, the way I like. There's a funny sea sponge I use to scrub myself. Only when I do, I notice the water starts turning gray. Then, to my dismay, I see pieces of gray shedding off my arms. Dead skin and Keri lotion. I try to swish it around, push some down the drain. That doesn't work. Then I hear my father's whistling coming toward the bathroom. He is a champion at this too. He can even whistle complicated classical tunes. And opera.

This is the part I loved, when I would stand and my father would pick me up, wrap me tightly in a big fluffy white towel, carry me out to the couch, where he would read to me.

He comes in and smiles at me. I love my father. I splash a little, hoping that will stir up the water, but I can see his eyes shift to the tub and register the ring. His eyes get narrower and his mouth twists up in one corner. He doesn't even look like my father.

"You're filthy!" he shouts. "Your mother is a goddamn fucking pig!"

I stare down at the water. Most of the gray has floated to the edges of the tub, which looks worse than before.

"I'm sorry, Daddy."

I am too scared to remind him about my skin. Back then, I had dry skin, "alligator skin," and sometimes layers would peel off when I scrubbed myself. He must've forgotten the dermatologists, the Keri lotion I had to use every day.

He stands there a few minutes, muttering. Then he pulls a neatly folded towel from the rack and places it gingerly on the bath mat. He pushes the faucet handle down so the water will drain. Then he turns away quickly.

"You're getting too old for the towel routine," he says, his voice quiet again. "Dry yourself off. Okay? There're your pajamas."

This doesn't feel the same. I use the towel to try to wipe the ring away once he leaves, but I can't get it all. Now the towel is damp, and dirty, but I dry myself the best I can. As I do, the cold air gives me goose bumps. I hate being cold. I wish I could go home early, sleep in my own bed. I don't even know where we are. All I know is my dad and his new wife live somewhere in New Jersey.

Later, we sit at the glass-top dining table. I keep my hands folded in my lap so I don't smudge the glass. I forgot to bring the Keri lotion, so my skin is prickly dry. Little flakes of skin come off my legs like dandruff, so I keep them really still. I feel very dirty, even though I'm bathed clean. I look at my father, and for a second, I blank out. I forget who he is. When this happens I trace number eights into the surface of the table. I just make sure to do it on the purple place mat. I loop them carefully, over and over.

When I look up again, my father is smiling. He is cutting a red apple into perfect wedges, all the same size. Slowly he pares the red skin away onto an apple skin plate. They drop onto it like tiny red parachutes.

"You know," he says in an intimate voice. It is the voice he used to use when he still lived with us and he told me made-up bedtime stories about Baby Bear and Mommy Bear and Daddy Bear. "Batsheva had a crush on me when she was a very young girl." He winks. "We went to the same summer camp."

My father arranges the apple segments like a flower on the plate. He places the knife just so, flanking the plate. Now he unscrews the lid of the honey jar, dips in a special spoon, and carefully drips it into a separate bowl. All the dishes match. Each item has its own plate, its own utensils. The cloth napkins are neat triangles.

"She wasn't happy when I married your mother."

My father picks up the knife, skewers one of the apple slices. Then he dips it into the honey. He leans toward me. I watch carefully to see if the honey will drip onto the glass table between the purple place mats.

"Batsheva doesn't like when I do this," he says. "Eat so late. You're a night owl too, huh?"

"Yeah!" I say. "I'm a night owl too."

I know, having read *The Goops* backward and forward— "The Goops they lick their fingers, and the Goops they lick their knives; they spill their broth on the tablecloth—Oh, they lead disgusting lives"—that eating a piece of apple dripping with honey off the tip of a knife is maybe not kosher. Not legal.

Not right. Not Batsheva-approved. This makes it all the more fun. A father-daughter secret.

My father leans in close to get the apple to my mouth. For some reason this all seems to happen in slow motion. All I can see is the white wedge of apple. The honey shining under the fluorescent light with a supernatural glaze. My father's smile, which I never noticed was lopsided before.

When I look back, am I imagining this scene was suggestive? Impossible. I was only five. And honey is just honey. Yet years later, when I was twenty-eight, I would travel through Israel sharing a hotel room with my father. When I was in college, he told me my mother never enjoyed sex, that she didn't know how to "get satisfaction." And though I was only five that night, a bunch of stuff got mixed up in me—stuff about dirt, and criticism, sensuality and shame, longing.

And the forbidden.

I'm ten. I live with my mother in Massachusetts. I took the bus by myself to visit my father for a few days. It's fall. I haven't seen him in a year. I was supposed to visit over the summer and take a trip with him to New Orleans, but he canceled for some reason. I think it was Batsheva. I don't think she likes me.

Tonight my father is taking me to my first opera, *Madama Butterfly*. I've already read the "book" as my homework before going to see it. It didn't make a whole lot of sense, but I'm proud I read the whole thing.

"You look nice," Batsheva says, staring intently at me. "Like you're going on a date."

"Thanks!" I say.

I smooth the front of my shiny satin shirt, pleased that she likes the new red corduroy gauchos and vest outfit my father bought me at Macy's today. I like clothes, bright colors, wild socks. I am skinny as a stick. But at least I don't have thin lips.

That's what my father says Batsheva has. Thin lips. Cruel lips. Not like mine or his. "We have generous lips," he said. "They have shape." That's what my father told me when we were getting a drink at Orange Julius the other day.

This means he's still my father and he sees something special and attractive in me that his wife doesn't have. I also have a middle name that begins with M, like he does. Mine is Miranda. His is Morton. He told me my middle name is from Shakespeare's *The Tempest*, but I haven't read it yet. My father and I are connected by blood and genetics forever.

"You're a pretty girl, aren't you. Blonde, blue-eyed. Must be your shiksa blood."

A warm feeling spreads quietly through me. I think this is the first time Batsheva has complimented me. I smile shyly.

I study Batsheva, looking for something to compliment. Underneath a brown wig I see a strand of her dull carrot-red hair. She is bulging out of a wool skirt and blouse, muscular calves and defined arms in sharp contrast to her fleshy bulk. Her lips are thin and pursed, her nose long and pointed. Splotchy freckles cover her face. Only her eyes sparkle. They are shaped like cat eyes, bright green with yellow flecks—her best feature. Before I can return the compliment, my father enters.

"Rachel, heeey, you look great!"

My father has come into the kitchen. I'm about to take a dramatic goofy bow, when Batsheva turns to my father. She barely comes up to his chin. I think she is five foot three. I am almost as tall as her. But she is as fat as she is tall. Only her fat is solid, and she is scary strong.

"Henry Morton Resnick, what is the matter with you? What the hell is the matter with you? You think I don't know what's going on? Do you?"

Batsheva's words shoot out as fast as BB pellets, loud and rapid. This is because she is supersmart, a doctor. My father is a librarian. He's supersmart too. But much quieter.

The smile fades from my father's face. He always slumps, but now he seems to slump even more.

"You come here," she says to my father. Then Batsheva storms back into the bedroom. My father does not look at me. Follows. The door slams shut, but I can hear scuffling.

"I won't stand for it!" she's screaming. I hear a thud and wonder what happened. Did something just fall? Are they moving furniture?

I sit down at the kitchen table, press my chair close to the wall. Try to blend in. I study the shape of the metal menorah in the middle of the table.

My father comes out first. He looks shaken. I wonder why he's holding his head funny.

Then Batsheva is in the kitchen, yanking the receiver from the wall phone.

"I'm calling my therapist. I'm going to tell her the truth. This relationship is incestuous. You two are sick. Sick! I want her out of the house. You hear me, Henry? I don't want her ever to come back."

I haven't moved. Now I'm pretending I'm in a game of statue. I choose a pose and I won't move out of it until the person who's "it" unfreezes me. I'm very good at focusing. And at games. I like to win.

Batsheva begins to dial the phone. Then she hangs up. Her face rumples. She pulls up a chair at the head of the table at the opposite end from where I am, sits down, and rests her head on her elbows. Her hips are so wide her flesh flops over the edge of the chair.

I look at the kitchen clock. The opera is at eight. It's six-thirty. It will take us half an hour to walk to the train, then a twenty-minute ride to Manhattan, then a ten-block walk to the opera house. We were supposed to eat first at a new Cuban restaurant. We aren't going to make it. I hold myself rigid. I don't like the red gauchos at all anymore. The length is stupid, the corduroy is too wide, the material looks cheap.

"What should I do?" says Batsheva from across the table.

She's looking directly at me. She's talking to me. Batsheva chokes back tears. Her wig is askew. It looks like a fallen bird's nest. More carrot-red strands of hair escape and spray around her face. I have an urge to laugh out of nervousness, but it passes. I sit up very straight, frown in concentration. Batsheva is still staring at me.

"Your father . . . " she says, then breaks down crying. "I don't think it's right how you are together. It's not right how he behaves with you, like you have secrets."

She shoots a look at my father. "Don't you have anything to say for yourself, mister?" My father's head is lowered. He's shaking his head. He's seated at the kitchen table too, in the middle, between me and Batsheva. In his hand is a fork he's fiddling with, pressing the tines so the fork flips up a bit from the place mat.

"Henry! Can't you even look at me?" she screams. My father straightens up, stares out the kitchen window with a deadpan expression.

Batsheva looks me right in the eye. I heard the word "incestuous" earlier. I know it sounds sinister, like a hissing snake. But I'm not sure exactly what it means. Though I know it has something to do with being the kind of daughter whose father can confide in her, and has maybe more fun with her than with his wife. Maybe if she weren't so religious then Dad would take her out for shellfish too.

"You see what I'm dealing with?" Batsheva says, weepy again. "He won't even respond. I don't think he loves me." I hear the pleading in her voice. I also feel it. Here I am at the table. There is my father. What do they want? A fear grips me: I don't want to be sent away. I don't know what's going on, but I know I don't want to be sent away from the house tonight, away from my father.

"Yes he does," I say. "Of course he does!" I can do this.

Batsheva smiles faintly. This gives me courage. I will be indispensable.

"Everything's going to be okay. Dad?" My father looks pained. "Don't you love Batsheva? Dad? You should tell her."

Some variation of this scene will happen many times during their marriage. Fighting, usually triggered by some comment over my appearance and my relationship to my father. Then a bizarre session of what feels like marriage counseling, in which my father slumps, his wife makes emotional, mysterious statements, and I pretend to know what she is talking about, and offer advice. If I pretend well enough, maybe she will let my father and me get on with our rare visit.

It didn't stop until I turned fourteen and Batsheva finally banned me from the house. And my father let her do it. I was staying at his house after another foster situation didn't pan out, possibly to live, and Batsheva must've freaked out and forbidden me to return. After this, my father placed an ad in a local paper, asking for a foster family that could take care of me.

Batsheva was wrong about one thing: There was no incest. But there was a lot of . . . confusion. Blurred boundaries. Acknowledgment of my sexuality, then rejection. Have an apple dipped in honey; you're a filthy little girl.

For my graduation from Yale, my father sent me a congratulations postcard. On the front was a picture of Lolita.

Four years after Winchester moved to New York, I pull out the one photo I have of him. He sent it to me during one of our breaks, when I said I wanted something to remember him by. It is a grainy snapshot from the shoulders up. He is casually dressed in a T-shirt and wears a gray beanie hat. I'm surprised by how vulnerable his large brown eyes seem, and how strangely scared he looks—as if someone is about to strike him. I never saw Winchester this way.

"You are beautiful," I say. "I hope one day you'll let someone love you."

Then I do something I've never done before.

You see, I save everything from my past. I accumulate because, for me, the past is so fragile. Parents can banish you, lovers can move across the country. Sometimes paper is the only proof that one has been loved.

I take Winchester's photo and I pass it through a lit candle so it flames brightly, curls, and turns to ash.

CHAPTER FOUR

Dark Prince, Part 1: Sex

1994

"My wrists still hurt from the cuffs," says Eddie Vaughan, rotating his wrists to revive circulation. This makes the tattooed yellow dragon covering his left arm jump through inky Japanese storm clouds. It also shows off his lean, vascular forearm muscles, which pop and bulge with the movement. Capable arms.

At this point, I don't think . . . good veins. I don't imagine leather belts wrapped tourniquet-tight around his arms. Or needles plunging hungrily into that same skin I'm now admiring . . .

I'm thirty-one. Eddie Vaughan and I barely know each other yet. We haven't wreaked mutual havoc for the two screamingly long years we're together. We are on a blind date at the Cuban coffee shop Café Tropical in Silver Lake when it still had waitresses with gold teeth and teased hair. Eddie has a fresh café con leche. He tears open a packet of sugar, dumps it in. Then a second packet. Third. Fourth. I'm mesmerized by the motion, the white grains, the excess.

"One sugar makes a Chevy. It takes five to make a Cadillac," he says, grinning. When he does this, the white scar on the right side of his face seems to twitch. It looks like someone pressed two fingers across the cheekbone and seared the imprint.

"What'd Jamie tell you about me?"

"That you were an amazing painter." And a real man, with testosterone to spare. Don't get thrown by the distinctive scar on his pretty face, she'd said, or be fooled by the ambiguous glam-rock look—he's a stud.

"She tell you I'm a convicted felon?"

"Must've slipped her mind. Are you kidding?"

Too late, I remember this girl once set her friend up on a blind date—and neglected to tell her the man was a dwarf.

"I have two strikes. Worst one's for armed robbery."

"Banks?"

I say this calmly, like I talk to ex-cons every day. Like it's the most natural thing. No way will I betray how much this unsettles . . . and excites.

"Mostly convenience stores, for smack money. We got caught robbing a porno theater when I first came to town from Texas. Out in Pasadena. Bad idea."

I pause, sip my own café con leche. With eyes lowered, I attempt to hide the surprise. I've never met an armed robber. Or someone with two strikes. Or an artist shortlisted for the Venice Biennale painting prize. For an hour, we've been talking about everyone from Lucian Freud to Tanizaki to V. S. Naipaul to Mishima to Kandinsky. I thought this man was a sensitive, passionate painter. Now I know he's an armed robber—and a former heroin addict.

"I love your tattoo."

"Covers up the track marks," he says wryly.

"Any kids?"

"I have a daughter, Devi. I named her after Rukmini Devi Arundale. Stunning dancer from India. Lotta soul. Revived *sadhir*, ancient temple dancing. She was also an early animal rights activist. Loved collaborating with artists."

He guzzles the leche, wipes the coffee from his lips, which I notice are not only full, but somehow lasciviously so. The scar highlights his exotic cheekbones and the tilt of his slightly Asiatic black eyes. I remember Jamie had told me his parents were an odd match: His father was a compulsive gambler who sold textbooks and his mother, a Japanese immigrant, was a housewife, a drunk, and a former bookie.

"Now here's a story. Her mother, Kristin, looked exactly like Nastassja Kinski when I met her. She was fourteen."

I blink. Eddie looks pleased. Utterly confident. He leans in closer. I notice beneath his polo shirt he has some kind of odd bumps on his slender chest, and I'm both fascinated and repulsed.

"She's the daughter of this former guru. An Indian visionary turned sacred chef. Her mother's a kind of casual mystic, too. Kristin had a bit part in this play I painted the backdrop for . . ."

He pauses. I am hanging on the words. In the pause, I imagine the affair, the beautiful teenage girl walking across the stage, the man watching her, drinking her up like she was a leche. Her bathing in this gaze. Finding herself in his desire, and on that brightly lit stage.

"She got pregnant. No way I was going to jail for statutory rape or some shit. So I abducted her. Took her on a Greyhound bus to New York City. She had Devi when she was fifteen."

I raise my eyebrows.

"Fifteen?" I sputter, even though I just imagined the whole thing.

"Her parents approved," Eddie says airily. "They're more enlightened than these uptight Puritan Americans. Other countries, cultures, they're more accepting of children and their sexuality. A girl this age, in Cameroon? She's already an old maid." He grins.

I am surprised to find myself wondering whether Kristin is the youngest girl he's ever slept with, and whether maybe it *is* all right. Then I think about what would've happened if I'd met this man when I was a young teen; at that moment I imagine I can feel his body warmth radiating from across the table.

"Eddie, you're more well-read than anyone I know and you didn't even go to college." Books I know a bit; drugs, not at all.

"What are you, my parole officer?" Eddie smiles. His long lashes flutter against his cheeks. He's very chiseled-looking, smooth and yet male, with fine raven-black Byronic curls. He wears expensive rose-tinted glasses, which sit low on his nose. When he speaks, he often peers over the frames, which gives him instant authority. So does his precise diction and his resonant voice. He intones, rather than speaks. There is something commanding about this man, even though at first sight I wasn't impressed. He didn't fit my predilection for either brash macho-man types or flawless pretty boys because of his facial scar and mysterious chest lumps. Not to mention that he's got twelve years on me. Now, after an hour, I can't take my eyes off him. Nor can I stop listening. His confidence, intelligence, and seductiveness are intoxicating.

I look down at my hands. My knuckles are torn up from boxing at the Y. I can handle this.

"Why were you arrested last month?" I'm thinking about his wrists bound by cuffs, imagining the metal cold and clamped around his skin.

"Some stupid clerical error, an old warrant from over a decade ago." I follow his cue, breathe a sigh of relief.

He tells me how he spent two nights in jail. On the bus over to the county jail, he was cuffed to a Mexican teenager who'd stolen twenty thousand dollars.

"This kid couldn't think of anything better to do with all that money but bring two 'bitches' to the penthouse at Disneyland Hotel and get caught. 'How about travel next time,' I said. 'Out of the country.'"

I laugh, as if I understand what he's talking about. I can't stop glancing at his muscular left arm with its tattooed sleeve. He, in turn, sneaks glances at my chest. His desire is palpable, thrilling. I can feel him stripping me naked in his mind.

Even then, I felt Eddie was a true outlaw. I sensed he could offer entrée into a world of abandon unlike anything I'd known, a world of intrigue and darkness, of mystery, outside convention. He would be my guide, if I let him. And we would travel, be seekers. For what, I wasn't sure.

Looking back, I recognize beneath the romanticizing lurked an ancient pattern of responding to men with secrets. Men with parallel lives. Men who lied. I thought at the time, here is a chance to enter that enigmatic world, maybe go where the men go when they leave. After all, hadn't my own father referred to himself as the main character in Thurber's "The Secret Life of Walter Mitty" when I was a wide-eyed kid and he was telling me about his affairs with other women?

"You should know, I still live with my ex." Pause. "It's just for convenience. Don't get me wrong. Also, I'm moving to Thailand in a month." Eddie leans forward, looking at me over his glasses. "I didn't expect to meet anyone."

The intensity of his gaze, it grips. He's . . . unavailable. I am powerless to resist this man.

"Hey, I took the bus over here from West L.A. Maybe you could drop me back at the bus stop?"

Second date: We meet for coffee at the Onyx, a divey hipster café in Silver Lake, two days after our first date. When we finish, Eddie wants to come hang out at my apartment. I let him. Again, we can't stop talking. When he leaves, five hours later, he kisses me in the doorway. This first kiss is so powerful he literally stumbles back toward the stairs. We look at each other, astonished. Suddenly shy as kids.

This is the instant superjolt we love junkies look for, mistaking it for destiny. If it happens, we are gone. Only now do I recognize the folly of such a chemical rush with a virtual stranger.

*　　*　　*

Third date: The first time Eddie strips down I am horrified. One minute we are sitting on the couch in my boho apartment. The next he has taken off all his clothes and is holding his cock in his hands, stroking it, looking at me with complete absorption, utterly unselfconscious. I'm, of course, transfixed—but also thrown off by his body revealed, if not his behavior.

Across his alabaster chest runs a thick band of rumply-rough dark skin. He looks like a burn victim who suffered a botched recovery. A fricasseed warrior on a day-pass from hell. (I will learn later part of this is true: he'd gotten caught in a house fire after he nodded out, and nothing could heal him because he turned out to be a keloid former, someone whose scar tissue forms hardened raised bumps.) Facially disfigured; his cock strangely shaped, its helmeted head flared like a small chubby parasol, and extremely hooked to the right; a corduroy chest, proud and puffed up—no shame here.

We have sex the first time. I do whatever he asks. It's that exciting.

Looking back, I realize I was already beginning to feel "turned out"—slang for when a pimp persuades a woman to prostitute herself. It can also mean convincing someone to change the way they think or live. Both applied.

One week later, I will write in my journal about the ravaged splendor of his body.

How quickly the delusions take hold.

Fourth date: We are parked on a side street in West L.A., making out like teenagers in high school. Palm trees throw shadows onto the windshield, streetlights shine dully through the glass.

"You taste like Starbucks," Eddie says, kissing me deeply and burying his hand inside my shirt. " 'Thou art skylarking with me—explain thyself, thou young Hittite!' One of my favorite lines from *Moby Dick*. Even though Starbuck doesn't actually say the line, it's Bildad, that's still always what I think of when I think of Starbucks."

We have just had a late-day coffee and now, somehow, we are in my car before he must return to the house where he still lives with his ex.

The windows fog.

"Double half-caf wet," he whispers.

I laugh. He stops my laugh with his mouth. His weight is so heavy, so male. Insistent and certain. Hungry. As we kiss, as we lock lips and tongues search with increasing urgency, he plants his hand between my legs and holds the hot core of me.

He will take me there.

The gear shift is grinding into my thigh. My spine is twisted. I don't care. Caramel slides through my veins, candy sugars my touch.

"Eddie," I whisper, throaty.

I am waiting, listening, for sweet words.

He leans back, sighs. He removes his glasses and places them carefully on the dashboard. I lean toward him, a plant arching toward sunlight. This gesture he does not seem to notice as he glances downward. What's wrong?

He quickly unzips his fly.

The movement is fast, confused. There is the sudden blur of pale flesh, the sound of thick jeans and skin, a chorus of friction. Eddie lets his head fall back against the headrest, then turns to look at me, eyes glazed and steady as he works. In shock, I think of me at age ten, rubbing sticks, trying to ignite fire years ago on the sand dunes of Cape Cod at a sleepaway campfire, the smell of grilling linguica and toasted marshmallows—anything but the scene before me. A scene that makes no sense. Our body odors rise, mingle, fill the interior of the economy vehicle.

Eddie Vaughan is jerking off in my car.

And I am not telling him to zip it up. Like this is typical early-evening post-date etiquette. Like I am not even here. My brain floats free from my heated body, hovers there up by the roof light, studying the man's movement, calibrating the number of strokes and intensity.

Then he grunts. All is silence.

A car rockets by, floods the interior with harsh white light.

After a moment, Eddie pulls me to him, kisses my lips as if we've just shared the most romantic date. I curl my hands into fists, crease my brow in displeasure. Still, his lips send currents through my viscera. I want to say something, but I cannot. Then he beats me to it.

"Rachel. Rachel. I need to see you again. Soon."

His voice shatters me. He called my name! He said *need*. Fists uncurl, open. I can *feel* it. His need covers my skin, burrows under, beneath. Calls to me.

This outlaw's need laces around my body like a cable-knit spiderweb, a delicate, unbreakable, magical cape.

When the car door slams shut behind him, rather than wake me, it seals the spell.

A few weeks later, he will move out of his ex's house and basically live in his car. I will ferry him and his twelve-year-old daughter around town. Some months later, he will be back in L.A. from Thailand, making half a million dollars creating commissioned artwork for various celebrities and power brokers. These people thrill to the hyper-real paintings depicting experiences they wouldn't dare—years ago, Eddie made his name on a series tracing the graphic tale of his relationship with one of his hookers and her mother, then followed it up with a suite of works inspired by his time as a teen male hustler.

Much of this new commission he will blow on hookers, exotic pets, costly watches, custom-made clothes, travel, gambling, and pharmaceutical-strength codeine.

But I won't know that. Because while I'm attracted to the double life I sense he lives, Eddie will keep it separate . . . and secret, until the end of us.

That is, except for the time early on when he invites me to participate.

I find this scrap of paper, written in the first weeks of meeting Eddie. Pros and cons, evidence, perhaps, of a willful delusion.

PROS: Intelligent, talented, committed, *great sex, travel, works out, iconoclastic, responsible, open, self-educated, follows through, creative partnership, supportive, good with animals, successful

CONS: *Anger (temper), financial sloppiness, irresponsible, bad manners, class chip on shoulder, *jealous/possessive, pushy

Memo to Rachelville: You call those cons? What about his history of heroin addiction, violence, conviction and jail time for armed robbery, former life as a pimp, male hustler, the fact he had a child with a fifteen-year-old he basically abducted when she was fourteen, disfigurement due to his own recklessness and drug use?

I mean. Jesus.

We are late for a party. Still, the Dutton's sign lures us both.

"Let's hit the bookstore," he says.

Books, books, books. We start at A. Both of us. Though I go to the fiction section first. He is more catholic in taste— sometimes starting in philosophy, sometimes poetry, sometimes history. Hours pass. We meet, as if reading the other's minds, each with a stack of books, a gleam in our eyes. We sit, talk books, ideas, read passages to one another. Who needs coffee? I can feel new tendrils forming, more synaptic sparks igniting my brain. He is a psychedelic hookah made flesh. I suck the conversational pipe, inhale, try to keep up with his visions. Only now do I realize that I made him my guru. The leader of our small cult of two.

"I'm buying you these books," he says. And I, always a sucker for gifts, for men who want to take care of me, accept.

I'd cultivated this habit for years with my father, always accepting his extravagant if unpredictable gifts of travel and financial support. It is something I'd learned to expect, and to think was my due. At this stage, I'd ignored the invisible strings that were always attached—with my father and with every other man.

At home, Eddie signs each book. "For Doubting RR, xxx EV" in one. In another, "EV loves you. Don't forget. You're mine."

Eddie is jealous.

We are at a party in Los Feliz. Anastasia is with us. It is the first time they've met. At the party, I run into a British journalist I used to have a crush on. Perhaps we have a mildly flirty exchange. Perhaps the British journalist looks at me too long. Or Stasia mentions offhandedly how much I used to like this man and Eddie hears.

Next thing I know, Eddie's hand is gripping my arm. Hard. "We're going."

"I'm not ready—" I begin, but his glare stops me cold.

As soon as we exit the house, Eddie steps close, screams into my face. Ignores Stasia, who stands awkwardly nearby.

"Who the *fuck* was that guy?"

A few people pop their heads out the window of the house where the party continues. "You okay down there?"

"Are you fucking him? Is that what's going on? Huh?" Now he's so near my face I can smell the root beer he drank. He doesn't drink alcohol; ex-junkies often avoid liquor.

"Rach," says Stasia in a small voice.

"Please, Eddie. No. I am not doing anything with that guy. All right? I'm with you. I only want you." And so forth. I pat his arm. Try to soothe what in retrospect was the first clear appearance of the raging beast inside Eddie Vaughan. I go on and on, pull gently on his jacket the whole time, move us down the street. More heads appear in other windows. Stare at us.

Finally we make it to the car. I remember thinking of it as a walk of shame. Something I'd caused.

Years later, Anastasia says to me, "Eddie was scary. Don't you remember that time on the street the first night I met him? After the party? I was terrified. I tried to tell you later that yelling wasn't right. I mean, I'd never accept treatment like that. I watched you try to calm him down, and it made me sick. I didn't recognize you. It was like the Rachel I knew, my friend, was taken over by someone else."

But back then, I couldn't see it.

One of our first phone conversations:

"I've been with men," Eddie Vaughan says.

"I've been with women," I say, challenging him right back.

Which is barely true. I went to Yale, a liberal arts college where everyone experimented with their sexuality, to some degree.

Eddie, though, when he says he's been with men, he means he's really been with them. Fellow gay male hustlers. Other junkies. Trannies. You name it. Sordid liaisons. Full-on relationships. "Fudgepacking," he calls it. Whenever need took over and a man was what was there.

"I want you to go to a girl, have sex with her, then call me right after, when you're still in bed together," he instructs me.

"Okay," I say, stunned. I mean, what am I supposed to say? I'm in so far over my head.

"Anyone recently?" he probes. "Is there any girl right now? I'm stroking myself, Rachel, are you touching yourself? Touch yourself."

Before I know it, I am having my first session of phone sex. Which is when I tell him about the yoga girl.

Next time we're having sex, he wants to know more about her.

"She's got a tattoo of a Koi winding around her ankle," I say.

"Yes," he says. "Yes. Tell me more."

He thrusts more deeply.

"When we kiss, I wrap her hair around my fist and yank her head back so her neck is exposed. Then I kiss her very slowly, seeking the pulse of her carotid artery, avoiding her lips until she cannot stand it and begs me to bite her mouth. Draw blood."

"Go on," he says.

At this point, no way am I going to tell him, "Er, actually, I've never even spoken to her. I just saw her in a yoga class and thought she was hot." I've gone too far. This fantasy's taken on a life of its own. He's taking me so hard, the way I like it. The way I need it. Break me in half, please. Penetrate my core. Batter the emptiness away. I don't want it to stop.

So I lie. I tell him about, um, Fiona. That's her name. Fiona from Australia. Yeah. By way of Perth. With the father's side tracing back to the Maori. Fiona, with the Afghan hound, and the leather pants, who never wears underwear, not even to church. Fiona, who likes to have me nibble her clit until the skin turns raw. That Fiona, with her tattoo of tears trailing down her neck, for the brother she lost to a drive-by. Fiona, who tastes like lemongrass and rock salt, tobacco and honey. Fiona, whose favorite color is green.

With Eddie I don't fake orgasms; I fake experience.

Fibbing leads me to unfathomable places. Around the globe. Doing things I can't imagine doing, with people I've never actually met.

Fantasy becomes not only integral; it becomes the only way we have sex. First there's the phone sex. Then his visits to the Circus of Books to find things for us: dildos, porn magazines, porn videos. I suspend all judgment. He tells me that he used to work for a porn mag called *God*—and that this magazine was strictly for pedophiles. "Beautiful naked kids," he says, "until the Feds found it and stamped it out." I feel dirty, hearing this. I feel daring.

I feel like someone else.

On the wall a video pulses glistening pinks and browns. I sip a watered-down vodka tonic, let the disco backbeat of "One Night in Bangkok" rattle my already rattled bones.

We are in Patpong, Bangkok's world-famous red-light district. Soi Cowboy, to be exact, a popular destination that's jam-packed with tourists. This is my first girly bar here in Thailand. It's my first girly bar ever, not that I'd admit it. Eddie has flown me here to visit him, three months after we met. He's been in Bangkok for one month. I don't know where he got the money for the ticket.

"I gotta hit the head," he says and walks off, grinning. Like he has a secret. I'm confused, but for a moment I bask in the swooning knowledge that this man desires me enough to fly me halfway around the world to meet him.

Then I get embarrassed. I'm now the only woman at the bar.

Instead of staring at the slim Thai girls in string bikinis working the shining silver poles, or the men staring intently at the girls like they're moving them around on stage with their eyes, I study the video on the wall. That's when I notice the video's no groovy moving Gestalt image like I thought.

It's a five-foot-high black penis sluicing in and out of a four-foot-high pink vagina.

While I watch, getting lost in the motion, the now lurid colors and shocking close-up, my whole body gets warmer, though that could be the tropical heat, the moist air that presses insistently on the skin like a groping hand. For a moment, I'm even more confused. Who am I?

I fight to dispel the anxiety.

This is my first night in Thailand. And Soi Cowboy is just a necessary stop on a daring tourist's must-see list. Everything's fine. I'm fine. It's all good.

"This place is beat. C'mon."

I don't ask where we're going. Eddie is a take-charge guy. A man who knows what he wants. He's been here before. Surely he knows the scene, what will be exciting for me.

Though at the moment, I'm having trouble putting together this Eddie, with the gleaming eyes and frantic walking pace, with the one who wrote me letters saying things like, "Thinking a lot about you. Imagining us in Thailand—imagining us in many different places . . . The thought of being with you, adventures, travel—the thought feels perfect. Astonishing how I miss you, my body—my heart, everything—this is so difficult. I miss you, Rachel. I dream of you," which I read and reread and even memorize. Oh, along with unnoticed or skipped-over lines like, "I seem to have enough codeine to preserve an acceptable comfort zone."

The next place we land is on a second floor, instantly seedier. Glamorous ladyboys, with thick eyeliner and luscious lips, go ga-ga over Eddie just outside the club. Have they met before? They seem to know each other.

"Hey, big boy," they wink, reach out and pinch at Eddie's nipples. His ass. He doesn't seem to mind. I don't know what to think. Is this normal?

"Are those real?!" they say, poking at my breasts in the tight-fitting halter top. I don't flinch because, I guess—looking back—I'm already numb. And we haven't even entered Firecat.

This time, inside, I pay closer attention to the girls. I'm a little more drunk, a little more primed. It's like I'm learning to play tennis. Catching on.

Back then, I wasn't catching on at all. I was thinking in terms of kid games, mild truth or dare. Do I dare? How far can I go? The man who believes I am a bohemian, a free spirit, a true artist—he wants to see if I can keep up. Step up. So I will. Eddie hadn't told me this game was serious. That there would be a steady escalation, with punishment for players who bowed out.

The girl I like is from Samoa. She's more muscular than the others, in her Catholic schoolgirl pleated skirt. Strong thighs and Doc Martens, hair in shiny black braids. Her white bra shimmering and sheer. Instead of dancing, she stomps around the stage, daring the men.

But she is not the one who shyly comes up to me during a break. It is another girl, slender as a sylph, her skirt loose around her hips, which jut out. Her bangs are like a silken curtain. She ignores Eddie.

I don't realize it at the time, but more than attraction, I am feeling protective. When she turns and offers her backside, I pull her to me, hands firm on either hip, press her thin body against mine. Run my hand down her slender elbow, tracing fine hair. I wonder, how the fuck old is she? She could be thirty. She could be thirteen. What am I doing? But I do not ask her that question then. I am numb. I am playing truth or dare. I am in a dream.

"Buy me a drink?" she says.

Eddie, who is eyeing me, and her, and the two of us together, goes quickly to the bar before I even have a chance. All of a sudden I am competitive. Who is he to cut in on this moment? She asked me to buy the drink. We are connecting. We are women. We understand each other.

I'm not aware of it then, but I am becoming unconsciously sensitive to the roiling hostility beneath the shiny disco beat. That the men want the girls, need them, but do not like them. Do not like women. Perhaps loathe women. And Eddie? Does he, too, hate women? I don't think that then. Later I will remember what he once said of his mother: "She was a drunken bitch." I had just chosen not to hear it.

Beware the men who hate their mothers.

I brush my hand through the girl's hair; she sways her hips against me. If I hadn't had sex already four times today, my first day in Bangkok, would I still be turned on? If I hadn't been drinking one vodka tonic after another, however watered down, would I still be responding to a stranger, a bar girl, possibly a prostitute? All the sex has gotten me so sensitized. So intoxicated. So . . . ripe. Even the sight of a leering ladyboy, or a sinuous monk, can get me going.

Eddie returns with her drink. Stands close to us. Puts his hand on her waist. Does he even see me flinch? She's mine, I want to say.

The girl takes the strange blue drink in her tiny hand, sips. What's supposed to happen now? Just then the lights blink on and off. Curfew. The music slows down. No more disco music. Now it's sappy good-night get-out tunes. Time to go. I breathe a sigh of relief. The girl kisses me sweetly on the cheek, glides through the departing crowd. I move to leave the bar, but Eddie? Eddie hangs back.

"Should we ask her to go get a bite with us? You know, at a diner?"

I look at Eddie. His eyes are shining. Has he forgotten I just arrived in Bangkok last night? That I was on a plane for thirty-plus hours? It's two A.M. I'm tired. Yet I hesitate saying it, not wanting to be the lame one, the party pooper. After all, he flew me over here. He says he loves me. Isn't it the least I can do?

Then I see my girl coming out of a doorway, in a cluster with other girls. They look so much younger in the harsh light. Teenagers. With a start, I note their school satchels with Sailor Moon stickers and smiley faces, tassels and bright bows. I can feel my face harden in, what, recoil? I can feel my face burn until it matches the heat in my loins.

"I'm tired," I whisper.

Eddie narrows his eyes at me. Scary. I don't really under-stand at the time how scary, even though I've seen an outburst before. I thought jealousy got him going, because he was so in love with me, and maybe insecure. What's this then?

"Just a bite. Aren't you hungry? Don't you want to ask her?"

Such a charming voice. Low pitched, persuasive, well-oiled. Why does this remind me of how some recovering alcoholics will insist you have another drink, because they want to see you drink the drink, imagining it is sliding down their own throats, warming their thirsty gizzards? Now I get stubborn.

"No." I shake my head.

I had to go back to the River City Guest House, with the pungent stench of urine rising up from the shoddy plumbing. Far from the Oriental Hotel I'd imagined Eddie would choose for us, with clean white sheets and clusters of fresh orchids. No. Any thought of complaining stuck in my throat, because wouldn't that seem spoiled? Eddie was the real thing. Grew up poor. Educated himself. Me, I had the most tenuous hold on self, and the most slippery grasp on what a partner even was.

Eddie is angry. I can feel it. The whole walk home on Sukhamvit Road, past signs for shark-fin soup and bear bladders, and roadside stalls selling Buddhist trinkets, he does not speak to me. Somehow I have disappointed him. I hurry to catch up, my sandals snagging in the uneven sidewalks. Outside the air-conditioned bars, my shirt sticks to my back. I am the ugly, sweaty American. Overly fleshy. Overfed. Overanxious. I am menstruating, and in the heat, at that panicky moment, it feels like my very insides are pouring down and away.

Back in the River City Guest House, Eddie has his face in the blood of me. Then he is pumping me against the lumpy mattress as if to punish me for holding back, for not inviting the bar girl to a diner. For chickening out.

Or is it that he simply cannot contain his desire for me. That it is so extreme, so strong, it spills over into girly bars, on the streets. Reckless.

Nobody has ever taken me this deep. It feels like he will come right out of my throat.

I have to plant my hand against the cheap plywood headboard to keep my head from slamming into it. From the angle I'm at, I can stare directly at the weird peeling strip of wallpaper bordering the walls above the bed—a series of Santas. Do they celebrate Christmas in Bangkok? Is Santa universal? It's August. I am having sex for, what, the fifth time this day? It feels like every orifice, every pore, is open and breathing, moist. Lava moves through my bloodstream.

A flash of light enters the room. On my back, I have a direct view of the doorway. A man stands there, framed by a cheap halogen light. He stares.

Eddie looks over his shoulder for a second. His face is covered in blood. Then he turns back, continues.

And I? I . . . keep staring at the man. As if this is the most natural thing, a stranger at the door watching me having sex.

Again, that dissociated, unreal feeling drifts in: Who am I? Minutes pass. Long minutes.

Looking back, hearing the Bangkok dogs bark again, the door quietly close with the man never having said a word—I thought I was exploring my secret perverse self.

Now, I see that I was out of my fucking mind.

*   *   *

I always wanted to make love on a moving train.

En route from Bangkok to Phuket. Sussurous click of wheels on the track, clacketing metal joints. I am on the top bunk. Eddie below. He came up to visit me at nine P.M. Felt how hot I was, but there were too many people. I try to read but can't concentrate.

Now he is back. It is eleven. I am burning up. He slips inside.

Olive green curtains drawn against the world outside gently swish against the bed. Metal hooks scratch softly as the train shifts, moving us still deeper inside each other, and when I get there, he claps his hand over my mouth, and I bite down on the fleshy ridge of his palm, the train rocking us to and fro, him grasping my hair and asking me, "Will you marry me?"

Pointing each word in the dark with his finger, even the question mark, drawing the words in the magical air.

"Will you marry me?"

I never dared really imagine marrying. Perhaps I never believed in marriage. Especially at age thirty-two.

My visions of marriage with Eddie—they don't get too far. A hypnotic montage of sex in exotic locales, from Zimbabwe to Bangladesh, tropical heat a constant, costly rings dazzling on our fingers, hearts aglow . . .

I don't really get to the part where someone has to go out and buy, say, a carton of milk. Or pay a bill on time. Or diaper a squawling baby. Or even smile at me consistently for more than a day at a time. Honestly? All that's trumped by a spotty vision of something I have not even seen.

At Drinks and Dreams, a beachside shack outside the Seagull Cottages, where we're staying in Phuket, Eddie feeds me a slice of papaya drizzled with lime. It is the color of sunset. The taste explodes in my mouth. Sensory overload. I take a sip of chilled chrysanthemum drink. Kiss. Can it get any better?

We're both wearing sarongs. Mine is wrapped around my body, while Eddie wears his around his waist. This is unspeakably sexy to me. A man, in a sarong, always at the ready. For me. His wife-to-be. Or at least, he's asked me and I am now savoring the question, making sure he really means it, and considering the answer if he does.

This is paradise.

I am in Phuket, in Thailand, halfway around the world from where I live, with a man who has just asked me to marry him the night before on a moving train, while he was making love with me.

Nirvana.

The sun heats our skin.

Eddie has a sore throat, stops talking for the day. Takes my right hand, writes in the palm, I WANT TO MARRY YOU.

I erupt in a disbelieving riff: "I don't believe you, I want to believe you, but I don't."

He takes my left hand this time and writes, I'M SERIOUS.

Then he kisses me, long and slow.

I still can't answer him. Something stops me.

A cool breeze blows faded rose tablecloths against our salty legs, edges of striped umbrellas ruffle at beachside, *tuk-tuks* putter. This is the backdrop to our blossoming romance.

Eddie takes my hand. Leads me to the water. The gorgeous sparkling green-blue Andaman Sea. We walk past Thai vendors carrying buckets and baskets filled with coconut and crudely chopped mango.

In the water, Eddie pulls me into his arms. I float. Weightless. And in his arms, in that moment, the Southeast Asian sun beating down, the beautiful water sparkling, time stops. I am in a state of bliss.

And I know, I am doing the right thing.

The whore's name is Bang, and she has a crush on me.

Later that night, at the Delight Ship Bar in the red-light district of Phuket, when Bang comes up to speak with me during a break, I roll with it. Why? I've been primed in Bangkok. And why not? I'm safe, aren't I? With Eddie Vaughan. He's practically my fiancé. Has he not asked me to marry him? He must believe in me. He must see me as a free spirit, one to match his own. Soul mates. I can do this. I can be open. Just like I am to his proposal.

Even though I prefer Bong, who's curvier, more lush, Bang is the one who fancies me. I even enjoy how the men glare, turning to me from the bar with narrowed eyes. One even spits in my direction.

"They hate you," says Eddie. Grinning.

"Let's blow this pop stand," he says.

And now here I am, walking hand in hand with a prostitute and my almost fiancé down the streets of Phuket.

In Seagull Cottage no. 7, we are all awkward. I hover above the scene. Again, if my body weren't completely opened to Eddie, if my heart weren't flayed also, I couldn't participate in this.

But it is, and it was, and I do.

We watch TV.

"Fanta?" he asks.

"Yes," I say.

"Okay," says Bang. We accept our cold glass bottles of orange Fanta, watch some more TV.

"Kiss her," he says to me.

So I do.

Soon Bang and I are kissing and tussling in the bed. Eddie watches, stroking my hair. Hanging back.

She is so small, tiny, in my arms. Against my body. I can feel her bones. Smell her. She smells like Laos. Pungent, swampy, foreign, and unbearably sweet.

Again, I feel protective. I want to make Bang feel comfortable. What do I know about prostitutes? Or whatever is going on here? Whatever she is? Only that they do not usually kiss. Nor come.

Okay then. I will make her do both. I will make this worth her while.

I will also show my virtual fiancé what I can do.

It is only looking back that I see how I compromised my values, every step of the way.

In the moment, though, I concentrated. I was an oasis, of sexual focus and prowess.

In retrospect, I was a mere fragment of a person. A mess.

Hours seem to pass, as I work her with my legs, rubbing her against me, not knowing what to do. Until finally, finally, she gasps, and pulls me close and tight. I try to ignore what has become the rank and potent smell of her. What I'm sure she smells on me: overdeodorized, hyperscented, strangely chemical American girl with doughy skin and fat breasts.

Still, she seems to like me. And after coming, she clings to my body, nestles against my chest. I look at Eddie. He is looking at me, though his eyes are vacant. My husband-to-be? Pulling desultorily at himself.

Bang sits up then. "I must go. My children," she says. She turns to Eddie. "You want fuck?"

"No," he says. "Nah."

He leads her to the door, pays her. Pulls out a wad of *baht*, Thai dollars, and pays her a sum I do not catch. Pays her for what we all experienced. What that is, I'm not sure.

She turns to me. Quiet. "Maybe I come visit tomorrow? Bring my children?"

I smile. "Yes," I say. "Yes, do."

But the next day we are back on a train to Bangkok.

The scent of the Laotian prostitute stays with me the whole way. Eddie's hand is between my legs. His anger from the second day—when I refused to ask the bar girl out to dinner—still feels recent and raw. And I wonder if perhaps, just maybe, just possibly, everything's moving a little too fast.

Even then, I was profoundly disturbed. I must've sensed something irretrievable had been exchanged during that transaction, something more valuable than *baht*.

I would not figure out what I had exchanged, what I had bartered, won or lost, until many years later.

We visit EVA airlines to see about changing his ticket to come back to L.A. sooner to be with me. And the office is closing, an hour before schedule. Eddie storms up to the last remaining clerk, does not grab him around the collar, but is close enough to his face to share the breath forged from a bowl of shark-fin soup. I stand to the side, frozen, but I see his eyes spinning. Note the veins popping in his slender neck, the nervous flexing of his bony fists as he screams at the thin clerk, who visibly withers, quakes like an aspen leaf, and I am completely . . . aghast. It is as if I have stepped onto the wrong stage. Into the wrong nightmare. Cast with the wrong people.

Help.

Yet when we walk away, Eddie takes my arm. Grips it. Says, "You are the one for me. Don't ever forget it."

And these words, the intensity with which they're uttered, I take all this—correction, I *mistake* all this for utmost passion. For, perhaps, the outburst of one who has tipped into a once-in-a-lifetime love—and is, what, disoriented? Prone to outbursts? They will pass.

Still, even then, it freaks me out. Makes me hesitate.

"I'll give you six months to decide," he says. "That enough time?"

At the River City Guest House, on the bed, the stench of the third world toilet permeating the room, which already stinks of sex and dirty clothes and humid moldering sandals, I find myself drawing back even more from what I call his "anger problem." Why should I promise monogamy to this man while I see what happens in the six-month period? Even as my man reaches for me, I decide to speak:

"I have something to say."

Long pause.

"Yes," he says.

"I would like to date other people. I'm not ready to get—"

Eddie springs up from the bed. I almost fall. Instantly, I grab hold of the edge of the bed. Get very still. And quiet.

He is standing nearby. Glaring at me. Eyes viral. Spinning.

"You bitch," he says. "Fuck you. You need to go home. Right now."

I freeze. Panic seizes me. Sweat seems to congeal on my spine, even though it is well over one hundred degrees.

I tear my gaze away, fix my attention on the title page of the book on the bedside table: *Divination in Thailand*.

"I'm going over to Fairweather's. Now."

He spits on the floor near me.

I do not move. What does this conjure in my memory banks? This is what I did when I was at the house on Polk Road, watching Angus Mathews beat my mother. This is what animals do, just before they are going to die, and they know it. They freeze. All fear drains from them. For me, it's sense of self that drains away.

This would happen again, years later, during Bukido training, when the instructor attacked me, began to strangle me, and I did . . . nothing. And knew. Finally. That in such a situation? Far from being the tough girl I imagine myself to be, I know I would've died.

Here in Eddie's hotel room, I give in. Freeze. Feel nothing. I take it all in. I am the wall. I am the Santas bordering the ceiling. I am . . . not here.

I don't know how much time passes.

When Eddie returns, he sits on the bed. This may be the moment before I die. And I will die knowing I did nothing to save myself. No matter. I'm calm.

I expect Eddie to pull out a knife. To break a bone. To wrench me. Stab. Strangle. Punch. Kick.

Instead, he places his hand, square, on my cunt.

"You're burning up," he says softly, voice husky.

I turn to liquid. Sex is my strength. Sex is my answer. I am always ready.

"I love you," I say.

And just like that, I am on the other side.

Because here's how the heroinlike love takes hold: Once I say "I love you," I'm done. Cooked. Finished. Strung out. It is like a sacred oath. Like fealty. It is the stuff of fairy tales, which I take more seriously than anything.

What I mean is, once I say it, I'm attached. Barnacles have nothing on me.

When he takes me in his arms, when he opens me up this time, and I am like a tropical flower nourished in tropical rainstorms, swollen and lush, then I know—I am bound.

At least for six months.

We are in the Big House—my brother, age three; me, age eleven; my friend Laurie Landis with the freckles and flowing brown hair and wickedly crooked nose, age eleven. My mother, age thirty-three, is out. I am taking care of my brother.

I remember the ages because $3 \times 11 = 33$. I have always loved patterns, sought them out. This one feels epic. It is a magic time. We are a family. Who needs a father? I am my brother's keeper.

"Take him outside if he wants to go," my mother says before she leaves. She looks beautiful in a navy T-shirt, her jeans, a wildly patterned silk kerchief around her kinky hair, blue eyes clear and full of life.

Michael is on his stomach, busy arranging seashells in mysterious designs on the Oriental rug, and shoving String up his nose. He's a real toddler multitasker.

I put the Jimi Hendrix album on the record player. Hendrix explodes through the sunroom, rattles the Baby Knockabout racing pennants that are nailed to the walls. Indian summer sun pours in through the bay windows.

Are you experienced?

"Wanna go outside?" I say to Michael, who is way too smart for his age. He looks at me slyly. Shakes his head no.

Laurie and I are sitting on the wicker couch in the sunroom playing cards. The cushions are covered with roses; the fabric faded from sunlight and salt.

"Blackjack!" she shouts.

"No way!" I shout back. "Laurie the Wicked Witch!" I scatter the cards like confetti. She scratches the win on the memo pad. We could play all day. Hours slip by.

A breeze floats through the screen door, brings a scent of honeysuckle and seaweed, along with the heavenly salt tang from Buzzards Bay only a few hundred feet away.

I stand up, stretch my skinny, tanned legs.

"Let's play a game outside," I say. "Michael, wanna come with us? Go outside?"

He gathers the shells into one pile, starts creating a new design, a kind of spiral.

"No!" he says. Flips on his back like a bug. His blond hair is a tousled, tangled mess. He looks like a roguish Italian cherub who tumbled out of a Renaissance painting.

"Well, all right then."

When my mother comes home, Laurie and I are finishing what must be the hundredth game of blackjack. I can still hear the waxy slap of the cards. Feel my bare limbs warm, folded up on those worn cushions, the satisfying bump of the wicker.

My mother comes in the sunroom. Gone is the kerchief. Gone the blazing smile. Her eyes are blurry, clouded. Exactly like how the sky gets when a squall is coming. She is drunk. Laurie puts the cards away. Her mother is a drunk too, so she knows what to do.

"Did you take Michael outside?" she asks.

"He didn't want to go," I say.

"Michael, did you want to go outside?"

"Yes," he says.

That's all I remember. Another day of babysitting. Right?

Later, up on the third floor, before Laurie and I go to sleep, I can hear the waves pounding the rocky beach. The sound of voices farther down, maybe at a barbecue. Laughter, drifting up the way it does near the water, like it's right next to you.

"That was awful, Rachel. She slapped you. And you cried."

"No I didn't."

"You did too. I saw you."

"No, Laurie. I did not cry."

No wonder I got yelling and love and responsibility all mixed up.

Now, these many years later, I'm thinking I did cry. How typical that I would have no memory of crying. She did slap me. I'm also thinking, my mother taught me well how to shut down. To take it. To disappear while it was happening. To drift away into the salty air, float over the pines, skim across the choppy water like a perfect flat stone.

Six months into the relationship, Eddie and I take a trip together to New York City. He has business. We will visit my father. This is big.

We are back at the hotel after meeting my father for dinner. Nighttime in the city. Urban lights prickle the skyline. Mirrors cover the walls. Eddie hikes up my skirt, takes me from behind. I feel his gaze elsewhere, look up and see him studying us, in the mirror.

"Look how good we look," he says. "Rachel," he whispers.

"What," I whisper back, expecting him to speak of love.

"I want you to pee on me."

Next thing I know, I am balanced over him, on the hotel bed.

"Is this right?" I say.

"Relax," says Eddie.

"I can't," I say. "The hotel sheets."

Eddie rises, pulls my hand. We enter the bathroom. He settles into the tub.

"Come here," he says. Still confident. Still succinct. Still so . . . focused on me. How can I refuse?

I don't say anything. Straddle him, naked. One leg propped on the ledge of the hotel bath. Everything smells so clean.

"I . . ."

"Shhh," he says. "I want to taste you."

Well, that shuts me up. I close my eyes. And slowly, to my surprise, a trickle dribbles down my leg. I hear Eddie open his mouth, slurp. He's so eager! This doesn't help; I clamp shut again. I think of waterfalls, of the Andaman Sea. Finally, I let loose a hot burst of piss. What did they say about Marilyn Monroe? She pissed like a horse.

Then, just as suddenly, it stops.

"I can't do this," I say.

Then I hear Eddie sucking, guzzling, slurping. Swallowing.

The stench of my urine is powerful. Sweeter than I would've thought. Also acrid. Undeniable. Catch this: the latest perfume. Topaz.

"God, Rachel. I want all of it. Everything. The last drop. More."

I don't remember anything else. I remember other times this was requested, and we soaked the sheets. And I didn't care. So focused was I on delivering the pissy goods, in seeing if I could release myself, if I could bow to his needs, if I could take the dare. Triumph. Overcome shyness, resistance, humiliation.

What I realize now, with this and so many other things—the sex toys he'd bring in his gym bag, porn mags custom-tailored to mentions I'd made in fantasy talk during sex (white trash boys for him, well-hung black men for me, juggsy women for I don't know who)—was that it was all part of the training to become his sex slave. It was like my body was a voracious learner, an intrepid sexual explorer, while Rachel and her brain lagged behind, split away, shut down—until the body took over. With each passing grade I earned, Eddie would offer more advanced levels of experimentation. After couples in mags, then there were the three-ways: two women and one man. I was amazed at how much that turned me on. We'd fuck. He'd fan these mags out on the bed. He'd look at them while we fucked. I, too, would study them. Recoil. Then they would worm their way into my brain, and stay there, and replay, and turn colors, and haunt, and demand reviewing, with instant wetness, and I would find myself wondering at, and shocked by, what turned my body on. When my brain repelled. Rebelled. And how my body always seemed to win in the end, like it finally had a mind of its own.

I still don't understand this.

At the time, I couldn't resist.

I felt like an initiate.

Eddie Vaughan was taking me by the hand and guiding me through a portal, into a seedy world I thought was inhabited, indulged, only by horny men. He was allowing me access to a world that many people played in but that I hadn't sought. I thought it was the true world.

And Eddie was one of its masters.

He saw through my uptight exterior, into the potential hooker inside me. The being who wanted nothing more than to fuck her brains out, to be compensated handsomely for it, and then to disappear—completely—obliterated by another's all-consuming desire.

*   *   *

Eddie has about him a bruised sadness, a kind of tough-guy-in-a-pretty-boy-shell vulnerability.

One day I arrive early at his downtown loft.

The door is open.

I find Eddie sitting cross-legged on the floor, playing a Mississippi John Hurt tune over and over on an old record player. Crying quietly.

"He kills me," he says softly, after a few minutes.

This is when my heart truly leaps to him. We are both wounded. I know now he is hurt inside; I will cut him all the slack he needs. I will forgive his outbursts. We will heal each other and find what we both lost so long ago.

In my fantasy world, it follows that love will triumph.

We are in a cheap motor lodge outside Palm Springs. One room, two beds. Eddie and I in one, his daughter, Devi, in the other. Most of the lodgers are truckers, hookers, johns. The courtyard is filled with noise all night, big rigs, fast-paced high-pitched chatter. Eddie draws me close. I freeze. I listen for Devi's breathing. Boundaries. The walls of this motel are so thin. It feels like my skin is permeable. Porous. When Eddie touches me I am helpless, even as he runs his warm hands insistently down my body, toward my waist, trailing what feels like sexual phosphorescence behind. Then I stiffen.

"Devi," I whisper.

"It's fine," Eddie whispers back in a honeyed, seductive tone, his words warming my earlobe, breathing into my body. I am still rigid, even with his hands seeking me.

"It's not right," I say. And for a moment, as I fight this growing center of sensation, I can once again hear my mother and one of her boyfriends groaning together through the thin walls of one of our rentals when I was a kid.

In the Palm Springs motel room, my sense of hearing heightens. Dry palm fronds scatter across the parking lot, mixing with urgent whispers. A car door slams.

"She's sleeping," says Eddie. "Relax."

I feel my body open to him. I hold my breath. Listen. I don't hear Devi breathing anymore. I don't hear the sound of sleeping. Do I? Then the roar of blood in my own brain, my body, drowns out even the sound of the big rigs tearing past outside.

And I give in.

I'm not proud of this.

I cannot give Devi back her innocence. I cannot return to build a boundary when there were never any bricks to begin with.

My appetites, my addiction, have not only damaged me; they have damaged others. Including children.

The realization is almost unbearable.

We are parked in a deserted lot in downtown L.A. We grab at each other, seeking deeper purchase, seeking answers to the stupid Hollywood party we've just escaped, seeking meaning. Eddie's hand is up my skirt. Working me. Frenzied fingers. Shame eludes me. Fog fills the strangely empty lot. It swirls around the still-running car, a piece-of-shit junker Eddie's therapist gave him, like that's what therapists are supposed to do. The same therapist said to Eddie, when he complained that I resisted some of his more outrageous ideas, "She should keep her anxiety in her pelvis." I extricate my arm from the tangle of us and wipe a spot clean on the steamed-up window. I shrink back when I see a man's face, leering, eyes shining in the orange dashboard lights. I look at Eddie, sure he'll defend me. Maybe even get out of the car, demon-fast, clock the Peeping Tom in the face. Instead, he leans over, across me, my trembling flesh, flushed body, heat rising. He beckons the man to the other side. "Cover up," he says to me. The stranger, lean and lithe as a wolf, lopes across to the other side. I watch him. I am numb.

Eddie rolls down the window.

"How much to see her tits?" Eddie says softly. "How much would you pay to see her naked tits, pressed up against the window, comrade?"

The man reaches into his pocket . . .

What you read above was a fantasy. Eddie's, not mine. He whispered it to me one night when he was fucking me in the ass, and he built on it each night following. I could easily see how, with one step, and another, I could become his whore. I could accept money for sex. I could lose myself that much. If I kept saying yes . . .

These fantasies—it got so I couldn't distinguish between what was real and what was not. I was in a constant state of arousal, a constant state of fear. Anything goes, or went. Until I said no. And he blew up.

One day, in bed, things were so tender. He was sad about his daughter, the time he'd missed with her, and I held him close. I felt him, hard, against me—something I could always count on.

"This time," I said quietly, "this time can we not have fantasy? Eddie, I want it to be about you. About us." So we did, for a minute or two. It was blissful, something buried began melting . . . until he said, grasping my hair, thrusting more deeply, "I see you with another man . . ."

In retrospect, it's clear he was stepping up the training.

"He's white trash. Young. Seventeen. Nineteen. Wearing overalls. Naked underneath. I pick him up on Santa Monica Boulevard, bring him back. You have been touching yourself, getting yourself wet for us both. I bring him into the bedroom and we look at you. Then you watch us kiss. I push his head down, he gives me a blow job. Then I fuck him in the ass, watching you when I come. You lie between us. I'll fuck you in the ass, then pull you back on top of me, stay inside, while he enters you from your pussy. So you'll have two cocks inside you. Do you like that?"

I do like that. Or, my body does. But does it have to be a male hustler?

I find myself cruising young men on the boulevard, surreptitiously checking them out at stoplights. They don't seem to notice.

This fantasy goes on and on, gets more elaborate each time, until one night he says, "Let me go get someone. Today, driving down Santa Monica, one boy looked at me when I was driving. I looked back. I drove around again, cruised past him.

He came to the window. I know where he is. I think you'd like him."

"Eddie, I didn't mean . . . a hustler? A kid off the streets? I didn't think . . . I was just, fantasizing, I—"

"Okay, okay," he says. And lets it drop.

But not really. There is always a new game. A new level. The next day, he mentions the personals. All the swingers. Reads me ads that catch his attention. Sees how I respond to that. I feel like I'm in a championship game, and I'm an amateur. And not only do the rules change daily, but the sport we're playing alters too. I can't keep up.

That doesn't stop me from trying.

Not yet.

Every day Eddie says, "five weeks and three days," "three weeks and six days," and so forth. Until we hit the six-month mark from when he proposed.

I visit Eddie in his loft. He has plans to take me to Pho 69, a fabulous Vietnamese restaurant in nearby Chinatown.

"Know what today is?" he says, looking like a little boy, despite his sinewy muscles. There is a softness in his Asiatic eyes, around his mouth. And an eagerness, like a kid on Christmas morning. Right then, I realize, I don't know why he cares so much about marriage. Why it means so much to him. All I know is, I can't say yes. The word simply will not come. When I even think it, I see this man losing his temper, his neck veins popping, his eyes narrowing, his voice like tires squealing on pavement, his fists tight and dangerous.

"Eddie," I begin hesitantly. "I'm . . ."

He comes over to where I stand on the concrete floor, near a puddle of dog piss. Zeno, the German shepherd puppy, is bounding around the loft. Wanting to play.

He takes my hand in his, starts to kneel.

"Eddie." I hold his hand so he can't squat down. Hold it stiffly.

"What?" His voice is still gentle but starting to peel at the edges. This pains me. I also feel my hands get clammy.

"I can't do this."

He yanks his hand away from mine, but stays invasively close. Now threatening. I can smell the oil paint on his hands, the pastrami lunch on his breath.

"I can't say yes to marrying you. Not today—"

"What do you mean?" he shouts.

I feel myself curling up, even though I stand straight. Curling up inside, like a pill bug. What's the script. Repeat the script. The words.

"I'm still worried about . . ."

"Yeah?" he says, his voice now harsh. Sandpaper. What grade? Grade one. Two. Getting thicker, scratchier, with every second.

". . . anger?" I say tentatively.

Zeno dashes by, and Eddie, too, is a blur of movement. Everything is sped up, and also slowed down. The dog is barking, and Eddie is suddenly halfway across the still almost-empty loft, hoisting his metal office chair clear above his head. For a second he looks like Atlas, a strange modern pose—man holding office chair aloft. Then he heaves it across the room. The chair smashes against the concrete wall. A leg shatters.

The chair falls against the paint-stained gray floor and topples several canvases. There's a great clanging. The dog leaps around. Barks. Jumps at Eddie's leg. He shakes Zeno away.

Then, slowly, like a periscope, he turns to look at me. And the gaze is as withering as any I've ever experienced. I feel skewered on the edge of his vision, the stake of his displeasure. I haven't moved.

"I just need some more time," I say. There is a long pause. Eddie curses to himself, a lavalike stream of invective, and I think of how the little girl in the fairy tale spoke and snakes and toads tumbled out. Then there is a long silence. Zeno scrabbles playfully around the loft, nosing a saliva-soaked pig ear.

"Please?"

Now Zeno holds a gnawed photo in his mouth. Eddie retrieves it. "That was my mother," he says.

"I'm so sorry," I say.

"What it is, what it was, what it shall be. Doesn't fucking matter," he says. "I hated her whiskey-soaked guts," he says. "She was a knockout though, in her youth. Got to give her that."

He studies the chewed-up photo. Shows it to me. His mother is fresh-faced, schoolgirl innocent with long black waves of hair, lush red lips, and lively black eyes. She looks like a forties Tokyo movie star.

"This is when she had just won the Miss Nippon contest. Just before she came to Los Angeles to make it on the screen. Instead she ended up modeling in Lubbock, Texas, at low-end car shows. Until that died out too, and she became a hard-drinking bookie. The American dream."

Eddie strides purposefully across the loft and embraces me. The hug is crushing.

"I want you to be my wife," he says. The ache in his voice cracks me open. "Even now, when I'm furious, can you feel how much I want you?"

Soon we are tangled in the dingy bedsheets, and he is fucking me incredibly hard. I don't even notice my stomach is growling. I think it's Zeno. Or, maybe, I don't think at all.

So when he pushes the new fantasy, how can I refuse?

It's the least I can do.

Only now, when I refuse, when I say I hit my limit, he will no longer attempt restraint in showing his displeasure.

I meet Ivana Gorsky in a hatha yoga class. I am here because Ivana has a reputation for unraveling even the most tightly wound students when she instructs. She is a cold, Baltic Russian waif—bone-slender, elfin with her delicate features, dark eyes, and spiky black hair like frozen tundra—limber as a gymnast. Strangely self-contained, like a spaceship. Or a mod kitchen appliance. She used to be married to a shipping magnate and live in China. They divorced when she refused to have his child. Ivana tells me during the break she is much more than a breeder and has no interest in ever procreating. I find her somehow otherworldly, supersmart, oddly expressionless. And yet she seems decadent to the core. I am weirdly drawn to her.

We exchange numbers.

Ivana calls, invites me to her surreal Cloud in Trousers salon, an informal gathering of avant writers and artists inspired by the poet Mayakovsky. I bring my boyfriend. Turns out she is a big fan of my boyfriend.

I didn't find out until much later that at that gathering she told Eddie he had changed her life. If I had known that, I might have trodden more carefully. But I didn't.

I invite Ivana to join the newly formed artist's group headed by Eddie. At this point in my life, I am still inviting everyone into my world—my privacy. I think that it's okay. Magnanimous. Not dangerous.

One night, after the artist's group, Ivana invites me and Eddie to go to a karaoke bar in Chinatown.

She lets Eddie take the wheel of her unwashed Ford Falcon.

Her spiky gelled hair shines in the bar's low lights. She orders a parade of clear liquid cocktails. When she sashays up to the cramped black square of a stage and sings Marilyn Monroe's "I Want to Be Loved by You," I can't tell whether she's channeling camp or coming on to us, or both. I'm confused. And tipsy. Eddie, his eyes on her, squeezes my hand. As usual, I am excited. The world is a sexual playground. Anything is possible, at all times. I know this. I know he knows this. But internal barricades keep springing up. The reluctant apprentice. I lack his polymorphously perverse, libertine vision.

I take the mic, sing Otis Redding's "(Sittin' on) The Dock of the Bay." Looking back, I cringe at the sight of me, at thirty-two, singing at a bar a song I'd only sung when alone before. Reaching inside for thoughts of my mother, who introduced me to Otis, trying so hard to impress, opening myself.

On the drive home, Ivana says, "I had a dream about all of us."

Now I know the energy's shifted. Eddie is driving. She is in the passenger seat. I had climbed in the back, eager to, what, be groovy? Accommodating?

Fool.

I lean forward. Eager. Buzzy. Exuberant with what I don't realize then is discomfort. Dissociation.

"We were all in a hot tub," she says.

"What were we doing in that hot tub together?" Eddie enunciates in that way of his. Seductive, supercilious, precise, louche. "What was going on?"

Ivana laughs. I giggle. And can't stop.

"It was like a seventies porn film . . ." she says, trailing off.

On the street, near where our car is parked, we three stand together. Awkward. I can hear the streetlights buzzing. We are in Little Tokyo. Everything's quiet. I stand before Ivana. Eddie is behind me. He doesn't even need to say anything. I already know what I'm supposed to do. I can hear his words from Phuket, echoing.

I kiss her.

Then it is like ring-around-the-rosey. Eddie is now to my right. We are in a huddle, like in rugby. Only not. I am still kissing Ivana. Whose hands are those seeking me? I'm already wet. A finger enters, and I open Ivana's shirt like I'm opening a theater curtain, move my mouth down to her breast, circle her nipple, suck.

We are *on a sidewalk* in Little Tokyo.

We are in a hot tub, steam rising, limbs entwining.

Suddenly, losing focus for a second, I realize with a start that my boyfriend is kissing her. Wait. My boyfriend is kissing another woman. A woman whose breast I am sucking. A jolt kicks through me. A frown creases my brow. I'm lost, unmoored.

Then Eddie takes my face in his hands, kisses me, and I relax. Or think I do. Or . . . Every second things are shifting. Kaleidoscopic. A moment of pretty-colored shards, dazzling—then cutting.

Eddie holds one of his fingers up to my nose and one up to hers.

"Smell each other," he says.

The sound of a shopping cart crashing by startles us all. Eddie now hugs us both close to him, protective. His long, lanky arms are big enough to circle us both.

"Hold on," he says. Unruffled. Brashly male. Confident.

Eddie moves across the street. Alone now, together, on the street, Ivana and I avoid each other's eyes. My head bows. I realize, looking back, I was ashamed. Stunned. I swing my head around and see it's Mason, the homeless guy who makes sculptures out of straws.

While Eddie is gone, Ivana and I do not kiss.

We do not touch each other.

We do not even look at each other.

When Eddie returns, he says, "Mason kept saying, 'Two women, two women. Man.' He wanted to know how come I got so lucky? How could he get so lucky? I gave him twenty dollars and told him to move on. That worked for him."

The spell is broken. I'm trembling.

"Let's walk Ivana to her car," says Eddie. Calm.

Before she gets in, she turns to us.

"I'd like to go on a date. With you both," she says.

I am standing next to Eddie again. We are a couple. Two people. Right? I cannot speak.

"We would love that," says Eddie.

"Bye," I say, lamely.

"I'll call you," she says, and crisply gets in her car.

I feel like I've just become the victim of a drive-by, but I don't quite believe it.

Almost instantly panic overtakes me. Which has been happening all along, whenever we push, when the fantasies become real. Yes, Ivana has been in our fantasies. Ivana walks in a bar, wearing a red sheath dress, naked underneath. And we three sit, sip piña coladas, kiss each other, our thighs touching, until we are feeling each other up in public—something that does happen at the Good Luck Bar in Silver Lake, with other people saying to us, "You all are so sexy." And I, rather than taking in the words, am tripping on, why is he facing her and not me? Feeling left out, and yet unable to say, please, can't we, maybe, just once, this time, have sex that is about *us*? With no fantasy? But no. No, there is always someone new. Someone from the support group meetings I go to for people who grew up with alcoholics, say. Like Candy, a crazy girl I've known for years and never thought about in these raunchy terms, although I always liked the way she played with my hair in meetings and gave me shoulder massages. A woman whose esteem mostly rests in her glorious breasts. Candy is given to saying things like, "I thank you. My breasts thank you."

I don't even think of her that way, until I tell Eddie this story and he says, "I'd like to fuck her. In the ass, that wide curvy fat ass, slap her tits, those big hanging tits, while you watch."

I want to say, stop, I don't want to hear. I don't really want to do that. That's Candy you're talking about. But I can't help noticing I get wet. How do I argue with my body? Why does my body respond? Maybe Eddie's right, and I am just straitlaced. Who's lying? Body or mind? I'm completely confused, and too ashamed to talk about it with any of my friends.

"If we make out with Ivana again, if something more happens, Eddie, will you promise me this? That you never ever actually fuck her?"

Back then, I thought this rule would save me. Would save us. Would keep what we had intact.

Silly girl.

"Of course," he says, embracing me.

Okay. I can take this on. I can cope with this. Hell, she's no threat. She's not that attractive. He won't fall for her. I won't fall for her. Sure, we can try this out.

Truth or dare.

Ivana invites us to her apartment for dinner for our first date. She lives in Atwater Village.

At the loft where Eddie lives, he doesn't even have a stove. He has a sink. And a minifridge. We eat out all the time.

So when we enter her apartment to the tune, the smell, of roasting pork, home cooked, both of us get dreamy. Domestic bliss, something neither of us grew up with, and both of us motherless now. Ivana bustles around the kitchen, sexy in an aloof yet slinky way, perhaps punk-kitsch in an apron, her blouse unbuttoned almost to the middle of her flat chest. Her skirt tight on her tiny, heart-shaped ass. Chanel red lipstick on her lips. We eat. The sauces dribble from our mouths. The triangular tension is palpable.

We are in the bedroom, on her bed. Red sheets, red quilt. A Bollywood movie plays in the background. We watch for a few minutes while Eddie runs his hand down her leg, then mine, then both. I don't want to be here, and yet, the juices are flowing. The energy is tripled, sextupled, exploding, unmanageable. Hindu chaos—many-armed, multiply tongued. I feel like I'm in the power of something I cannot handle, at all. Like Pandora's box has been unlocked. Like I'm being swarmed. Split open. Spilled.

Or, I am in a seventies porn film. Like Ivana predicted. Or orchestrated? Who is choreographing whom? It is Eddie who is the painter of this scene.

At one point, both Ivana and I are lying on our backs, naked. Open to Eddie as he plunges his fingers into each of us.

"I want to fuck you both," he says huskily.

I shake my head no, reminding him. He catches it, enters me, thrusts deep, while kissing Ivana. Somehow, as long as he is penetrating me, as long as he's saving that most sacred act for me only, then I think, oh, I can manage this. This can be controlled. This is just—what—us expanding our horizons, us testing boundaries, us working out how we can be together, keep it alive, forever. Fuck. Me. Harder.

Looking back, I was kidding myself. Already deep in denial. Throwing everything over for that love-heroin sex-saturated hit.

After he fucks me and comes, I am superaware of every time he reaches toward Ivana. Touches her. Kisses her. Spoons both of us, with Ivana closest to him.

I freak. Go outside, sit on the stoop, smoke a cigarette. Go numb. Do I think about what's going on in there? I can't handle the energy. The fear. The . . . I'm not thinking. I'm sitting on the stoop. That's all. Concentrating on smoking.

It won't be until much later that I learn what happened every time I ran away. To go smoke. To buy tomatoes. Whatever.

How do I know? She was a singer, and wrote songs about it all. Performed them in local cafés and clubs. So I learned. And choked on that learning.

One evening, after the torrid first date at Ivana's house, we all meet up at the legendary bar-restaurant Chez Jay. With its cut-rate nautical theme, beer-soaked floor, Hollywood history of quiet trysts in dark backrooms, anything goes.

"I'm falling in love with both of you," Ivana says.

We are sitting at a booth with a plastic red-checkered tablecloth.

I hear what she says: she loves *both* of us. Not just Eddie, but me too! My heart revs and spins. At the same time I am busy wondering if my boyfriend has his hand on her leg underneath the table.

I am jealous.

I am turned on.

I am in over my head.

"I would be honored to be with both of you," says Eddie.

I look at him sharply. Is he serious? I did not sign up to be married to two people. I shift uncomfortably in the booth.

"What does that mean, like, what, we all get a house and move in together now? Is that what we're supposed to do? Is that what you're saying?" I blurt out before I can even think. I'm so disturbed. Sometimes I talk a lot when I'm agitated.

They ignore me.

They ignore me, and yet I choose not to leave.

Even when the two of them carry on a lengthy conversation while I just sit there, a conversation that ends with Eddie staring at Ivana adoringly. Then he says to her, "I'm a genius. You're a genius."

Still I choose not to leave.

"What about me?" I say instead.

Eddie turns, considers me briefly. "I don't know. You might be a genius too."

Looking back, I realize I hadn't "hit bottom" as they say in twelve-step meetings. I was nowhere near ready to give up my love drug—especially when its potency had tripled. No matter how toxic.

What's a love junkie's favorite way of not dealing with reality? Denial. I could not bear the truth, so I would lie to myself through fantasy.

I could not bear to believe that Eddie would break the rule we'd set, or that he would cheat on me, let alone that he would fall in love with someone else. Didn't this man want to be my husband? Didn't he swear he loved me every day? So I chose to believe he was faithful and constant.

That left Ivana. She was the question mark. If I could control her, all would be well.

Solution: I would fall in love with my biggest threat. After all, love was always the answer for a love junkie.

So, after we three make out another night at Ivana's place in Atwater Village, to the sounds and manicky flashing sights of more Bollywood flicks, and Ivana whispers in my ear, "I love the way you kiss me," that's when I choose to fall for her.

My rationale: I will participate in a ménage. On the surface, I will play with the woman in bed—only for the purposes of pleasing my man.

But the fantasy I create is that Ivana and I will forge a secret bond—right under Eddie's nose.

Ivana will love me, and I will love her. We will be the best of girlfriends, and that way, she will never cheat on me. That way, she will never fuck my boyfriend behind my back.

If anything, hell, Ivana and I can be together, just us two. Leave Eddie out. This is my plan, in case Eddie steps out of bounds, breaks our rule.

This way I imagine I've covered every worst-case scenario.

So when it all blows apart, and nothing goes as planned, I'm devastated.

We are in Eddie's loft.

"I want to fuck you both. I want to fuck Ivana. I keep thinking about it. I'm so turned on. I've been sketching for a new painting . . ."

"Eddie, you promised."

He stands up abruptly, smashes his fist on the desk so the books and papers and tubes of paint jump around. Zeno barks wildly.

"You can't stop this. You can't forbid me from fucking Ivana."

"But we have a rule! We agreed!"

"You're a square," he says disgustedly. "I thought you were a bohemian spirit, like me. I thought you got it. Turns out you're totally uptight." Then he says something I never thought I'd hear:

"I need a break."

"Are you breaking up with me?"

"I'm just saying I need a break."

During the two-month break, I keep thinking about how "square" and "uptight" I am. This plagues me. He's found me out! My sense of self is so tied to his sense of me, I can't let go of him. Can't move on.

Unless it's with Ivana.

I keep contacting her. E-mailing her occasional romantic notes, full of oblique yearning. I let her have her distance, let Eddie have his. We are all single, sorting things out.

Eventually Eddie comes back, saying he wants to try again. I'm hesitant. I decide to hedge my bets, keep in touch with Ivana too.

I write her yet another bright and cheery note, saying I hope she is working through our experience, getting clear.

Eddie agrees to go deal with his anger in therapy, to make things work with us.

He's so willing, and loving, and calm—it makes me suspicious. Even if I don't allow myself to put the whole picture together.

Instead, I get bolder with Ivana. For the first time, I proclaim my "true feelings" in no uncertain terms in an e-mail: "I can't stop thinking about you, Ivana. I think I'm in love."

Her response comes quickly. Like a dagger. The words venomous. As if spat through cyberspace. What I recall is something along these lines:

Do you really not know the role you played in Bitchfest '96? Is it truly possible you are blind to the fact that I've been fucking your boyfriend behind your back for the last four months? First he trashed you like an unwanted disease. Then he dumped me and went back to you. Now you keep contacting me. You're either aggressively stupid or just a willful bitch. Go away.

I read that note, reread that note, reread it again. My blood runs cold. Then hot. My face flushes with shame, and rage, and fury. Homicidal fury. I never imagined—always it is a failure of imagination, or perverseness—that they were getting it on the whole time.

Duh.

Everything focuses into a sharp, small point. I become a living switchblade. Ivana is dead to me. A devil doll. A wraith. A succubus. I dial Eddie's number. I hate all women. Even more, I hate all men.

"I just got an e-mail from Ivana," I say. "She told me everything. Eddie? I am going to kill you," I say. Then I hang up.

This concentrated fury, this utter hatred, is somehow cleansing.

Eddie calls back right away. Says she's a bitch, a psycho, why would I believe anything she said? She is insane.

"Let's go to couples therapy," he says. "I love you," he says. "More than life."

After the ill-fated ménage—the infidelity, the horror—I develop a new habit. I pick at my lips, tearing dry skin away. Eddie will find me sitting on the busted-up couch in my boho apartment, picking away. Unaware. And he will say, every time, "You look like a moron doing that."

I will look up, stare with baleful eyes, keep picking. I am a broken woman. A fraction of what I used to be. If I keep picking at my mouth, making myself bleed, somehow, everything will reassemble. Right?

One month later, I move in with him.

CHAPTER FIVE

Dark Prince, Part 2: Death and Insanity

1996

Looking back, it seems ironic that he wanted an open loft but clung to a secret life. It seems doubly ironic that I was working as a private investigator for a small Silver Lake firm but couldn't recognize severe drug, gambling, or prostitution habits in my own home.

We lived together there for one year.

It was the year of hell.

We had not had sex since the "incident."

That's what we called the affair Eddie had with Ivana Gorsky without my knowledge—not the ménage. The part when they hooked up and I wasn't around.

I still didn't know how long it had lasted. Or how it all happened exactly. Which meant I had tons to chew on. To imagine. Replay. Get paranoid about.

This was the way it was when we chose to move in together.

You might say this was inauspicious.

You might say this was barking mad. Or at least masochistic.

I am at home in my office, on the phone. The door is closed.

"Stasia," I say.

"Rachel, I can barely hear you. You sound awful. What's going on?"

I shift around in my chair, swivel my back to the glass door. "I can't talk loudly. He might come in. He does that, Stasia. Just comes in. Unless I lock the door, and then he knocks until I open it."

"Rach, I'm worried about you. I haven't seen you in weeks."

"I know. It's okay. We're just going through a rough patch."

"What I mean is, I don't see you anymore. Are you getting out?"

"I have so many cases for work," I say. But the truth is, I sit and stare at these cases. I can't bring myself to make the calls, count the hours, do the reports. "I don't know what to do," I say, sighing. I check furtively over my shoulder. He's not there.

I glance over at the tiny window. It offers a glimpse of blue sky, just a sliver. There's no oxygen here in downtown L.A. The window opens onto the four-foot-wide backyard, what used to be a loading dock. In what used to be a bread factory, which is now luxury lofts for artists. Ours is two stories, and an architect used to live here. The space is airy, sunlit by two-story-high glass facing east. Behind the loading dock, there's black bamboo, a brick wall—and beyond it, a ruined building rising like a ragged urban castle, branded with angry graffiti.

There are rats outside at night. Enormous city rats. They scuttle along the loading dock and steal Zeno's dog food.

Men generally like lofts. They like the space. The open air. The lack of privacy. It was Eddie's dream to live in a loft. I agreed to move in to this new, bigger loft only when he promised to have two private offices built. I insisted on the one with the window. The larger room. He'd betrayed me. He owed me.

Just like my father did.

Little did I know, that office would become my prison.

"Don't you want me anymore?"

We are in bed, on the second floor of the loft. I sleep close to the cinder block wall. There is a hole in that wall that opens into the parking garage. Afraid rats will come through and ravage me, I've stuffed chicken wire and fabric in the hole. This also helps keep out the chill of L.A. nights. Eddie's warmth used to help with that too. Not since we moved in together. We've hardly had sex. Who's punishing whom? He's so close. I can almost recall what it feels like to have him hold me, suck my breasts, fill me up.

"Jesus, Rachel," Eddie says. He turns abruptly, rolls away from me.

"I don't understand," I whisper. "Eddie, I know things are hard—"

"I can't do this right now. Fuck. I need to sleep."

Except he has insomnia. How is he sleeping?

I turn on my side, my back to Eddie, arch away from him, face the hole in the wall and let warm tears trickle down.

*　　*　　*

One time, I have to get a book from Eddie's office. Right on the floor near where I find the book, I see an open black leather bag filled with empty white bottles with white labels. Pharmaceutical-strength codeine.

"I found those bottles."

"What were you doing in my office!"

"What about the bottles?"

"You fucking bitch. Stay out of my office! Stay away from my stuff!"

"Eddie, are you taking codeine?"

His voice softens. "No, Rachel. Those are really old. Relax." He pulls me to him, hugs me close so I can feel the corrugated lumps of his chest, his heat, and his ardor. I live for rare moments like these. And just like that, I forget that all the labels were dated from the past few months.

"Watching football is masturbatory. I'd rather do that than spend time with you," Eddie says.

After a few months, Eddie is pulling in the dough. Any time a juicy check comes in, we are on a plane somewhere.

I get so used to him paying for big-ticket items that I quit my P.I. gig. After all, I still believe the sum he owes me for his bad behavior is beyond calculation. "I didn't sign up for this," he protests. "I'm not your daddy." But, I am ashamed to say, I argue it is only fair.

We fight so loudly neighbors hear us even through thick concrete walls and floors.

Meanwhile, when we aren't fighting, we both seethe.

Travel is the only relief.

* * *

For months we plan a big trip to Morocco. We will go for four weeks. We read books in preparation. Buy clothes. By this time, Eddie is supporting me entirely—under duress. I am trying to write. I am close to finishing my first book, a novel. Eddie is making twenty times as much money as I am then able to make, with his Hollywood art commission gigs. His bold autobiographical art exploring his sexual fantasies and experiences is gaining an even more fanatic following. He got ten thousand for a painting inspired by the stranger-finding-us-fucking-in-the-car fantasy, which he dashed off in only a few days—tops—and never touched up. He just has to find assistants to run errands and buy paints and canvases, since I will no longer oblige. To me, the logic seems obvious. After all, doesn't he want to take care of me and prove his love?

Never mind the hostile vibe between us.

I write in my journal, two weeks before we go to Morocco: "Not all of this is my insecurity and depressive nature."

But clearly, I believed I was insecure and depressive, and causing Eddie to pull back.

Then I go on to say, "I am, in a word, miserable. Sick. I can't take being yelled at. Anymore. I am filled with doubts—enormous discomfort, with the man I live with, at the place I live in! This is wrong. Something is very, very wrong. I am in hell."

One day before the trip, I write, "Still in hell—what will the trip bring? All unreality anyway. In misery. Deeply."

The plan is to fly to Paris first.

I am wildly unhappy, yet somehow I convince myself the trip will be romantic. How could it not be? Paris, City of Light. Me and my boyfriend. En route to a monthlong adventure. Together. The Champs-Élysées, croissants in bed. Then Morocco, a country neither of us have visited. A chance to reinvent everything.

We get off the plane. As usual, I have overpacked. His friend Jim Knox is there to meet us. He is tall with gray hair and wearing a black leather jacket, black boots, and shades. An aging hipster. An actor and rabid conspiracy theorist.

"We will enter Paris like proletariats!" he declares.

Jim does not offer to help me with my baggage, even though he is carrying nothing. Eddie has his own, much smaller bag. He has just one. They do not seem to notice me dragging my bags through the charming cobbled streets of Paris.

"Can we get a taxi?" I say meekly.

"We don't need a taxi!" yells Jim. "It's not far. We take public transit in Paris. These people are civilized here. We will take the bus, then the metro."

"Fuck the rich," says Eddie.

"This is really heavy," I say to Eddie.

"So's mine," he says. "We don't need a fucking taxi."

I shut up.

By the time we arrive at the hotel near Saint-Germain, I am sweaty, my shoulders and back ache, I have blisters, I am wretched. But then, looking back at this time in my life, I was wretched before I even came on the trip.

At the door, Jim says, "Nice hotel, eh? You want to get your knees knocked, Eddie, there's a spot right next door."

I realize he is talking about whores. In front of me. I think, how rude. But when I think about it now, it is all so much more than rude. Try degrading. Try the clue that Eddie still visited whores. Try massive denial.

I don't remember much of Paris. We were barely there. It was expensive.

I do remember visiting Notre Dame.

I insist.

At first, I resist the long line of tourists pressing greedily, coldly, single-mindedly, to enter Notre Dame, but I know I must go in.

I am squeezed, thrust forward, deposited before the worn wooden rail facing the spectacular triptych of stained glass windows, and there is a mass in progress. Incense. Ancient stone floor worn and grooved from so many thousands of feet. The priest in bright green. I begin to weep, warm tears, mindless of the elbows, the feet, the hands pressing and pummeling. I weep for my mother, for my lost youth, for the past. The priest leads a song. I pray for my mother. I tell her, "I love you, I hope you're in peace, and if not, I'm trying to help you get there, Ma." The hymn ends. I step away and light her a candle for ten francs.

I step outside to where Eddie is waiting impatiently. I don't try to tell him about what I just saw. Despite the tension between us, Eddie does hold me briefly when I say, simply, "I was moved, thinking of my mother." And tear up.

Eddie is red-hot in Hollywood right now. Upon our arrival at the hotel in Casablanca, he calls his art dealer, Dale Valentine. Valentine tells Eddie a young Chandler scion bought one of

Eddie's recent paintings of a ménage gone bad in triptych for a cool million, and on the strength of that he got the Getty Center commission for a series of paintings in the same vein. And he can plan it out from Morocco.

The second night in Morocco, the noise from the bar across the street is earsplitting. The sign says BAR AMERICAN/GRILL-BAR/BELLYDANCING. All night there are sounds of relentless Arabic music, talking, and what seem like fights. One man gets thrown out of the bar. I go to the window. He strips his shirt off in the street and commences to howl.

I turn back to make a comment to Eddie, but he is out cold, a shadowy lump on the bed. On the floor beside him, a half-drunk bottle of cough syrup.

"Hi, mister," says the boy to Eddie, speaking a surprisingly fluid and fast English. "You are from America, yes?" He points at his filthy Mickey Mouse sweatshirt. "I love America! Mickey Mouse!" I am used to the men ignoring me. Not boys. Then he glances at me, flashes a smile, before swinging right back to Eddie. The boy's eyelashes are astonishingly long. More like fringe. His good looks don't match his scruffy clothes.

We have just arrived at the Hotel Batha in Fez. We haven't even gotten our bags out of the taxi. The engine is chuffing black smoke, shaking as it idles. This boy is on us like white on rice, as Eddie would say. He's unusually young for a hustler. Clearly precocious.

The boy scurries around to the trunk, heaves our bags out even though he is small. He can't be more than ten years old. There's something Dickensian about him. Wily. The taxi driver yells at the boy to shoo him away, but Eddie puts up a hand, places a wad of *dirham* in the hands of the driver, who speeds away.

"My name's Abdul," the boy says, smiling broadly. His teeth are a blinding white. Brown eyes large and expressive, dark curls soft and loose around his finely featured face. Lithe and stylish in a grubby way, with a red scarf wound around his neck, he could be a child actor. A gypsy charmer. His sweatshirt is so dirty you can't see Mickey Mouse's eyes. "I will carry these to your room."

"Why aren't you in school?" says Eddie. I look at Eddie, whose eyes are focused on Abdul. Does the boy remind him of himself? Of his daughter, Devi?

He is a beautiful boy by any standard.

"I am twelve," he says. Then hangs his head for a moment. "I can't afford school." I roll my eyes, but Eddie leans in closer.

"That so," he says gently. "Smart boy like you?"

"Come!" Abdul says cheerfully. He hauls the bags, somehow, up the marble steps of the hotel. The hotel staff squint at the boy, and tell Eddie, "This boy is no good." But Eddie shuts them up. "He is carrying my bags," he says to them, raising his voice. "You will be nice to Abdul." Unused to his edgy tone, they drop the subject. But I see the staff whispering to each other and shaking their heads.

The next morning, as soon as we exit the hotel, there is Abdul. Waiting. He is eager. Barely able to stand still. He is wearing the Mickey Mouse sweatshirt again. With him now is a tall, pear-shaped man who sweats profusely.

"Brahim," he says.

"My brother," says Abdul, who looks absolutely nothing like Brahim. The whole thing seems utterly suspect, but Eddie doesn't seem to notice and I figure, what do I know? He's the one with street smarts.

"We tour medina," manages Brahim.

Entering the medina of Fez is like entering the medieval.

Everywhere, tableaux. Everywhere, donkeys. Everywhere, donkey dung, filth, hidden passageways, meat hanging on hooks.

In one passageway, an old man in a camel-colored djellaba, dirty white pointed slippers, and skullcap, heaves a young boy up against a cedar door. We can hear the sound of his body hit the wood. His skull thuds. The boy cries.

"He's a crazy," Abdul says to us. "The boy, he tease him. He threw something, so the crazy, he punish."

Brahim is not one for such nuances. He is giving a "tour," so he will stick to the main landmarks. He will point, and he will hurry us along after only a moment.

"Dit one I name, Kairaouine Mosque. Fourteenth century," says Brahim, pointing.

We turn another corner and enter a small triangular courtyard. Young boys kick a deflated soccer ball. Everything is dim. Narrow. Close. All lit faintly by electric bulbs, the exposed wiring tacked up on walls.

We enter an unlit passageway. There is an old man with a cane, blind, tapping his way through. We step aside.

The smells. Donkey dung underfoot.

Abdul and Eddie are deep in conversation. Abdul holds Eddie by his hand and arm. They look like a father and son.

A woman crouches in the corner of a passageway, her head bald, her eyes sealed and unseeing. She is singing something, holding out her hand for alms.

Abdul catches up with Brahim. Eddie falls into step near me. His eyes are shining. "That boy is a genius," he whispers to me. I look at him sharply. I'm so jealous in the fallout of the incident. Even a boy can stir me. "Lemme tell ya, that kid works his charm and his intelligence."

"I don't know . . ."

"I want to send him to school in the States. I'm going to work something out. Whatever it costs," he says to me. I am stunned into silence.

As if Abdul senses my discomfort, he drifts easily back to where I am walking. Then, he takes my hand and arm. And something melts in me. What if he were my child? As if reading my mind, Abdul says sweetly, "Like my mother," tugging at my hand. My doubts evaporate.

Looking back, I see clearly how Abdul played on our vulnerabilities. Our paternal and maternal instincts. Perhaps he also played on other fantasies. Eddie was someone who always needed more, more, more. To always escalate. He was insatiable.

We set out to a café for breakfast. I wear a sequined scarf. They say sequins keep the somber spirits away. Anything to dispel the suffering I wear like a full-body-and-face veil.

"Let's sit in the sun," I say.

"I want to sit in the shade," Eddie says.

"Can we sit in part sun and part shade? I—"

"God fucking dammit! What is wrong with you?" Eddie stands up, knocks the table askew. A glass falls to the ground, shatters. His face is red. The Muslims around us shrink back. One couple leaves. "I'll get my breakfast somewhere else. Away from you."

I order *nous nous*. An almond croissant. Wear a brave face. Write in my journal. Try to stop trembling.

Later he is more jovial. Maybe he found some codeine. "I guess Muslims aren't used to people losing their temper, huh?" he says genially.

"People at home are scared by your temper too," I say. Eddie laughs, as if pleased. I don't know what to think anymore.

I reach out to him, and for once, he lets me. He draws me to him. Kisses me. I can't help myself; I have to know and before I can stop it, the words fly out: "Tell me again, that you weren't with Ivana the whole time we were having trouble, that—"

Eddie gets up abruptly. Spit flies from his mouth as he speaks. "Fuck off. Just fuck you, Rachel." I brace myself. This, I've heard before. Then he launches into something new.

"You're crazy. You're insane. It's uncanny how much you're like my mother. You don't stop talking."

The truth was, looking back, I was insane. I went insane. I chose someone so unsafe, so threatening, so unpredictable and emotionally abusive—perhaps insanity was actually the sane response.

The truth is, I later learned this compulsive behavior is one of the hallmarks of a love junkie. I was so desperate, so needy, I couldn't even embrace one moment of peace. I had to pick and poke at it, always wanting more. I was a middle-aged infant, famished for a kind of unconditional love that was no longer my due.

"I didn't mean to . . . I just—"

"I want to break up. We're leaving tomorrow for home. I want you to move out. I'll pay for an apartment."

"Do you still love me?" I say later, hunched into a ball on the hotel bed. Very still. I don't know where these words come from.

"I don't know anymore."

"Can't we think about it?" I say. "I don't want it to be over." Helpless to stop the words.

"I'm going out," he says. Slams the door.

I stay curled on the bed. Cry. Then, unsure when Eddie will return, I read a slender book, Silvia Perera's *Descent to the Goddess*. I'm instantly transfixed when I come upon the description of the woman under the influence of Ereshkigal, the fallen sister.

Eddie comes back, smiling strangely. "Get dressed, jesus, get out of bed. We're going to have an authentic Moroccan meal. Abdul and Brahim have invited us to their family's house for lunch."

I am mostly terrified. Deep down I don't believe that Brahim is Abdul's brother. So what, then, is this family? And why would we willingly go to the heart of the medina, which is full of hidden threats and unknown dramas, into a house of people we barely know, who are clearly hustlers?

But the play is already in motion. Half an hour later, Brahim and Abdul are at the hotel. Not inside, because they are not allowed. They loiter just in front of the steps. We pass through

136

the lobby. The hotel staff looks at us with narrowed eyes. As if we too are scum.

Abdul is wearing his Mickey Mouse sweatshirt again, but on this day, it is turned inside out. At first this strikes me as poignant. Then it creeps me out. Once again, as if he knows, he takes my arm first, leading me jauntily into the medina.

We reenter the medieval. This time, we take winding passageways I do not recognize. The light seems to get murkier. There are green plastic roofs overhead, protecting the merchandise, the meats laid on tables covered with flies, the carcasses hanging from hooks, twisting in the green-cast muddy light, as we press on deeper. Finally, we squeeze through a passageway all of us have to wedge ourselves in, except for Abdul, who darts through easily.

We enter a tiny room with barely any furniture, just a cot and a piece of fabric on the floor with a steaming pot of couscous, from which I know we will all eat with our hands. The prospect repulses me. On the wall hangs a picture of Johnny Cash cut out from an American magazine. On top of the television, I catch a glimpse of a photograph. It is Brahim and a woman. There are no group family photos. None of Abdul. Suddenly I am certain this is a scam.

A woman enters with the dishes. She is all smiles. But her teeth are small and pointy, and her body language loose, and I wonder, is she just some prostitute they hired? What is real and what is not? Will I make it out of this hovel alive?

The anxiety of being there, stuck, and having to eat what might be poisonous—or at best, disgusting—takes over. I don't remember much else. I make a show of eating a little couscous, spend most of my time eyeing everyone suspiciously, watching Eddie light up every time he speaks with or watches Abdul—concentrating on keeping my stomach from flipping in circles. Eddie eats lustily. He has several helpings, while I claim an upset stomach and eat little. Smile a lot.

While I watch Eddie chew long tendrils of gristle and soft unidentifiable meat, I feel something darker and uglier than I've ever sensed with Eddie.

Somehow we make it out. Brahim and Abdul leave us at our hotel, ask what tour we want tomorrow. Eddie says, that's enough. Brahim's brow darkens and Abdul's handsome boy's face turns sharp and feral. What strikes me in this moment is, Abdul is not a boy. He's a hardened man, at twelve years old. And we have just fallen off our carefully polished hook, slipped off like two stupid wealthy American carcasses, onto the filthy streets of Fez. Their masks are gone. What I see is pure, unadulterated hate.

I see this hate in another pair of eyes.

Whenever Eddie looks at me.

Our last night in Fez, we eat a pizza at Ville Nouvelle. Eddie seems depressed, troubled.

"Brahim and Abdul wanted me to come to their house again tonight," he says.

"Huh? Why?"

"Abdul wanted me to come by. Said he had something for me." Eddie looks at me. "It's like South Central, or Bed-Stuy. Ghetto. I refused. Things got ugly."

"I don't get it."

"They made other suggestions, and I turned them down."

I don't know what he's talking about, but my skin is crawling. This is the first I hear of "suggestions." My brain lurches to an image I had of Eddie sitting on Abdul's cot while the boy knelt before him and sucked his cock. Then I blink it away. What do I know? I could just as easily imagine him with a donkey. Any creature seems a threat when you believe you are worthless.

The next morning, Brahim and Abdul, and another large, thuggish man, are waiting outside for Eddie. He sees them from the window. Seeing him nervous, I feel the love surge up in me, like bile.

"Where are you going?" I say when I see him heading out. "Will you be okay?"

"I'll be fine. I just have to pay them for the 'tours,'" he says. But he seems scared. Something I've rarely seen. "I'll be back in a few minutes."

I watch them from the hotel window. Eddie is against a wall. The two men and Abdul surround him. At first I think they are talking. I worry things are not going well. My heart is pounding. I'm just about to go downstairs when Eddie returns.

"They took my jacket."

"What?!"

"I didn't have enough money. They were mad I cut the tours short."

"You look pale."

"They wanted my shoes too. I said, no way; you can have the jacket and five hundred dirham."

I know there is so much more to the scene, wonder what this is really about, but Eddie is visibly shaken. And quiet. I decide to drop it, to go to him, comfort him, embrace him. We make love for the first time that whole trip, that morning, in Fez. And just like that, I am comfortable again, drawn by the chemistry, back in the fantasy saddle. This will last until we return to Los Angeles: a kind of uneasy, unhealthy, and twisted détente.

Back in Los Angeles, Eddie paints the backdrop for a short play inspired by Shakespeare's *Macbeth*. It is to be performed at an evening of plays called *Daggers in the Smiles of Men*. He also collaborates on one of the pieces by telling the writer/director, Richard Fitch, observations from our recent trip to Morocco.

When I sit in the audience, fanning the program on my lap, I have no idea what the play is about, or what Eddie has painted.

The house lights go down. The stage lights come up. It is clearly Morocco. Minimal set, spiked by a painted minaret. A pot of tea on a low table. An Arabic archway. A cloth hanging. A man and woman in Western garb, another man in the telltale djellaba. He looks eerie under the stage lights, his face partly in shadow, like the Grim Reaper. There is stylized haggling. The mock pouring of tea. Then the woman speaks, and what she says reminds me of something I said on our trip to Morocco, and I shiver. The man snaps at her. She falls silent, turns away, walks upstage. The two men lean close, whisper. Something exchanges hands. Money?

Darkness falls, followed by a strange crimson glow. This is Fitch's trademark. Blackouts segueing into red light between scenes, à la Bergman.

When the light comes up, the woman is gone.

"My wife . . ." says the Westerner.

"Your wife," spits out the Moroccan.

"She pleased him?"

"The sheik was well pleased, yes." Somehow, as the oblique dialogue unfolds, it becomes clear: The husband sold the wife to a wealthy, perverse sheik who used her, he and his men, raped her repeatedly, then murdered her. And wrapped her corpse in a carpet and disposed of it—somewhere in the desert where nothing can be found.

Blackout.

No blood on the stage, but the blood in my body freezes.

"How'd you like the backdrop? That minaret?" Eddie asks me, eager. We are home. In our downtown loft.

"Magical. The light falling on it was luminous. You even manage to make a minaret sexy. I don't know how you do it."

"And how about my first collaboration with a real playwright. Did you like the Moroccan play?"

"As a writer, I loved it. Like Paul Bowles crossed with Shakespeare and Orson Welles." Eddie smiles. My heart is pounding.

"As your girlfriend, I have to tell you I was upset. And frankly, terrified."

Before I can even get the words out, Eddie slams his fist into the wall. "It's fucking art!" he screams. "You psycho—it's a play. Fuck me." And he stalks off, turns on the television. Basketball. March Madness. "Shannon?" I hear him on the phone with his bookie. I retreat into the office. At least there's a lock on this door.

*   *   *

141

One day many months later, on our return from a strained trip to Trinidad and Tobago, I am in the bathroom and Eddie enters. His lanky shadow fills the doorway.

"I'd like to kill you," he says. And walks out.

Soon after this, I find myself in Eddie's office, snooping. I know how to snoop. I am a female P.I. I am a spy in the House of Love.

This time, I am looking for something that will help me move out. Because I am stuck. I know I have to go. I don't want to die. And now I'm scared.

Maybe some part of me wants to die. To join my mother. Or at least visit.

The stronger part wants to live.

I can't yet find the stage door, the exit. But I finally want out of this play.

Then I see them. A thin sheaf of envelopes sticking out of his black leather day planner. I look around. Unsnap the clasp. Trinidad and Tobago stamps, Caribbean cheerful. Addressed with a childish hand, full of loops and ink blots, curves and swirls. Shaking, I open one. Another. And I remember the night Eddie insisted on going out to gamble when we were in Tobago.

We'd been fighting in the hotel room. "Who did you have a date with?" he kept asking. He was obsessed about something that occurred before I visited him in Thailand and before we were committed to each other. I kept refusing to answer. One, because it was a celebrity. Someone maybe I still thought crazily might be in the picture, should Eddie and I break up. Or at this point, maybe it was more the principle of it. I was not going to budge. I wanted to hold on to this small square of privacy, this little fantasy.

Eddie wheedled, he pleaded, he screamed, he whispered. He would not stop asking. For hours. Until I was teary, exhausted, but stubborn. I went to the bathroom to pee and he chased me, shoved me against the wall. My whole body tensed. This is it, I said to myself. I have never let myself be hit, or shoved, ever, by any boyfriend. This is over. I'm out of here. I'll endure until we fly home, then I'll break up. When I'm in my country, safe.

He stormed out. "I'm going to gamble," he said. I stared dully at the television, tropical sweat moistening my skin even with the overhead fan slowly slicing the heavy air. I fell asleep, tears streaking my face. When he returned, he was gentle. Sweet. Fucked me fiercely. And I didn't think about anything else.

Until I read the letter. And see this line: "Remember how I was, and how you left me." All the other lines about money, about wanting to visit the States, about Tobago—nothing stays clear but this line. And the whole night opens up. The stained bed. The tiny room in a beachside blue-painted bungalow. A voluptuous full-bodied Caribbean girl with gapped teeth, one gold, sloe eyes, a mass of heavy hair, long scratching nails, a well-worn, educated hoochie.

Quickly, I take the note back to my office, make a copy, and return it, shut the door to his office.

I think about incidents he's told me. How his exes intercepted letters from other women. Psycho women who invented relationships. Who were jealous. Who wanted to stir up trouble. Never was Eddie in the wrong. Never was Eddie unfaithful. But didn't we sleep together when he was still living with his ex? I wonder now if she knew what he was doing. If she thought they were still together.

I wonder what I'm getting out of this. Do I like the degradation? Am I conducting an experiment in survival? Does this drama excite me? How much can I endure? I keep thinking, and getting nowhere, and repeating the line from the Tobagan woman over and over: "Remember how I was, and how you left me."

When he returns home, he comes into my office, where I am sitting numbly in a swivel chair. "I saw the letters. From that whore in Tobago. I hope you haven't gotten me infected with something."

Before I can react, he lunges toward my chair. Grabs the sides of the headrest.

I don't want to die, I don't want to die, I don't want to die, runs through my brain.

For a second, I imagine him slugging me. Or squeezing both sides of my head until my brain pops out. I have to get out of here. Violence was never in my plan. Or so I told myself.

Looking back, I see this relationship as being like a transfusion: I gave him light; he gave me dark.

Or at least that's how I like to think about it. The truth is, we traded light and dark.

He was using drugs, women, gambling.

I was using him.

Together, we were just a couple of junkies.

"You motherfucking bitch! What have you been doing? Snooping in my office! That's just some woman—she was at the hotel, a friend. You are insane. Insane."

But this time, I knew I wasn't. I had the note. Copied. I don't know why this was the proof I needed, after having accumulated so much else.

I guess I was just . . . ready. Ready to give up. Ready to admit defeat. Ready with whatever tiny bit of strength I still had left to return to the light.

Ready to live.

Or so I thought.

I left him.

CHAPTER SIX

Henry and Michael

1991

In the year 5751, according to the Jewish calendar, my father takes me on a first-class trip to Israel.

How does he pay? He cashes in his IRA fund.

"It's my two-week retirement," he says, grinning.

Outside the Tower Air terminal, I am startled to see what my father calls luggage. Clearly, he has not traveled anywhere beyond the Poconos, to the summer bungalow colonies where Orthodox Jews gather, for decades.

"I don't need to check anything," he says to the porter. Then my father gathers his overstuffed blue plastic bags around his legs. On each bag, ECONOMY CANDY is written in bright red letters.

My father loves his chocolate. Economy Candy is the dusty cut-rate candy store on the Lower East Side of Manhattan where he gets his monthly supply. Before it got discovered, before the rents skyrocketed, the Old World Jews ruled the

Lower East Side. One of them was my father's beloved grand-father Mordechai, who made good in the *shmata* business selling children's "rompers." When the neighborhood changed, he moved across the river to Jersey. But his grandson still wanders the Lower East Side.

It is also where my father first used to travel to buy Judaica books. Worn tomes purchased with money given by his grandfather, who wanted a grandchild of his to become a rabbi and carry on the holy learning he revered even though he himself was a businessman, a man of money, in the New World. His grandson, thanks to his grandfather's encourage-ment and love, developed a passion for the texts. For the bold right-to-left flow of thick ink, the music and power of Hebrew.

I stand apart from my father curbside at JFK airport, present my passport, check my Tumi suitcase. All the while, I'm thinking, Who is this man? The two-week trip will be the longest time I will have spent with my father since I was four years old.

When my father invited me on this trip a month ago, I couldn't resist. What better way to get to know each other, to repair the past, than to revisit the place I was born? What more fitting location in which to celebrate my father's fiftieth birthday? It promised to be an adventure. A reconciliation. And a shared milestone.

The idea was not just to celebrate his half century on earth, but also his impending divorce from Batsheva Klein. The marriage he now called a twenty-two-year mistake.

"To think that I spent all that time with a woman not of my style," he liked to paraphrase from Proust's *Swann's Way*. The remedy: a two-week retirement.

My maternal grandparents weren't too happy about my mother's marriage to Henry Morton Resnick. Granted, once the Jersey Jew got Janie pregnant, they encouraged the union. They glossed over the information that their middle daughter had already spent a little time at Austin-Riggs, the posh sanatorium near Boston, after she got kicked out of Wellesley for having an affair with an older professor and subsequently suffered a mental breakdown.

So when a very pregnant Jane and Henry were about to board the transatlantic ship in Boston Harbor for a new life in Israel, with their one steamer trunk, the parting was tense.

"Here," said her mother, Emma Tottleworth Fitzgerald, handing Jane a small package.

It was a bar of soap wrapped in a five-dollar bill.

Jane's Irish Catholic father had no gift, but he had something to shout out once Jane and Henry boarded the ship:

"Just remember, JESUS CHRIST IS GOD!"

I guess Jane did remember. Because at the last minute, she did not go through with the ceremony that would've sealed her conversion to Judaism. Which means, technically, I am not Jewish, since the mother determines the passing down of religious pedigree, even though I am a sabra, a native-born Israeli.

Sabra is the Hebrew word for prickly pear; supposedly sabras have personalities like the fruit—tough on the outside but sweet on the inside. I don't know about that, but I do know I would've been sent on the train to Dachau in Germany. In that way, I identify strongly with the Jewish aspect of myself. Culturally. And thus as an outsider from the WASP, Christian mainstream. Where things get sticky is when I have to face that I am also a stranger when it comes to my own Jewish cultural heritage; I know so little about the traditions, the texts, the history or language. I am an outsider on both sides of my blood family: The quietly anti-Semitic WASPs see me as Jewish, and the Jews consider me a shiksa—an unabashedly disparaging term for a non-Jewish girl or woman. In this way, I can't win. So I don't try.

On the plane, Dad translates articles from the Israeli papers. He shares literal meanings, puns, and underlying metaphors. Most of it is lost on me. Still, he goes on and on.

"I get frustrated, Dad," I say. "I only got as far as those Hebrew alphabet cards I had as a kid."

I don't say, "when you left," but that's what I mean: When he left, I was four, and had a stack of Hebrew alphabet cards and one Hebrew alphabet book. All I remember from those years and those books are the first four letters: aleph, beth, gimel, daleth.

"That pains me," he says. "I don't want to burden you further. Make more complications."

"No, Dad, it's an adventure!" I say, patting his knee, my heart filled with an unexpected, pure-feeling love. "I'm here with my own private tutor, I read all the books you suggested, and now we're going on a field trip!"

Looking back, I realize I was in a familiar addict stage.

Manic, in anticipation of a trip to a foreign land, where reality could be left behind. Including a fantasy where a feeling of love, connectedness, fusion, was on the way. I was the one who had too much baggage.

Here is one of the news items he chooses to translate:

An Arab-Israeli in West Jerusalem yells, "Allah is great!" and stabs a man with a double-edged knife. It is the first time someone with an Israeli citizenship card has perpetrated an act like this, the first time such an incident has occurred in the center of Jerusalem. He stabbed the first man, was accosted by a Yeshiva student, and stabbed him too.

A woman asked him, "Why?"

And he stabbed her.

When we deplane in Tel Aviv, the day before my father's birthday, I notice my father has a smear of brown on the front pocket of his baggy pants.

"Dad," I say, pointing.

"Ah, forgot I had a chocolate bar stashed there," he says, smiling gently.

For some reason, this breaks my heart. If I had a washcloth, I would lean over and clean the stain. What did my father tell me about our ancestors? We come from a long line of foot washers, a tribe whose duty it was to cleanse the extremities of learned, holy men.

How does my father fit into this ancestral line?

Henry "Hank" Morton Resnick. A modern-day Levite. A kid who had all the promise in the world when high school ended. A scholar-athlete, handsome, brilliant, recipient of

New York City's Outstanding Private Basketball Player Award his senior year—especially unheard of for a Jewish boy.

Here is my father now, the shlumpy assistant librarian at Klau Library in Manhattan's Hebrew Union College, the man who somehow has never been able to complete his dissertation in Judaica to obtain the Ph.D. from Columbia, the man who's spent over two decades in an unhappy marriage. He holds tight to his ten plastic candy bags, finding solace where he can. Greedy and careless, letting chocolate bars melt in his pants like a little boy.

A little boy about to turn half a century old.

On the bus ride to Jerusalem, we pass the small two-story building where I was born. "Twenty-eight years ago there were no other buildings here," my father says. "It was isolated, on a barren hillside. Your mother found it. Dr. Carmel, that was the doctor who delivered you. She specialized in troubled cases."

I don't pursue this.

We arrive at the King David Hotel. Lech Walesa is there too. Cops are everywhere. I can't contain my excitement. Here I am, with my father! At long last! Together!

"It's my father's fiftieth birthday!" I say to the porters, to the front desk clerks, to random guests.

One friend says to me, years later: "You know the thing that gets you in the most trouble? Exuberance." I wasn't sure what he meant. This might be an example.

"Rachel," says my father in the lobby of the King David Hotel, visibly annoyed. "Stop."

This is the first sign of irritation so far. I choose to ignore it.

"In '63, you couldn't even enter the Old City," he says, changing the subject.

The next day, my father goes to visit his eldest son from his second marriage, Reuben, at the yeshiva where he has been studying for a year. I go to the walled Old City, with its twisted streets and ancient dwellings. I'm drawn to the sense of age, and of mystery.

I enter the street called Omar Ibn El Khaittab, step into the heart of the Christian Quarter. I pass dark stalls, men in turbans, women in white veils, bags of jewelry spilling onto carpets laid on the stone street, tiny kebab stands where meat turns slowly on skewers, flames leaping. After angering some women at a fruit stall by trying to take a photograph, I turn quickly onto Armenian Orthodox Patriarchate Road, follow the wall in the Armenian Quarter. At this point, I do not know that the bones of Jews are buried in those walls. That each time the Arabs take over, they ransack the Jewish cemeteries, use the stones to build. I am alone on a long stretch of road and wall. I am wearing baggy shorts, a tank top. There's no one else on the road, and I'm beginning to feel alone. Which is when I see him, in the distance. The religious man. He is very thin, almost wraithlike in his brown hat and long brown overcoat. As he comes closer, he visibly shrinks back. Shields his face from me, and, like a crab, turns toward the wall and continues to walk in a northerly direction, so as I pass him, his back is to me.

I stop short. Unclean, I think. And I remember another averted gaze: my own father's.

*   *   *

It is springtime on the East Coast. My college roommate Christina de la Torre and I have just returned from spring break in Florida. En route back to New Haven, we decide to stop at my father's house in Teaneck, New Jersey. Nobody's home, so we drop our bags on the porch and wait. We are giddy, suntanned, and loose from a week on the beach.

Then we see my father and his family in the distance, walking single file up the sidewalk. They are dressed fancy. And it hits me: It's Saturday. They must've just gone to synagogue.

Batsheva is first, leading the family conga line. She's terrifyingly regal in a thick wig and a wide-brimmed felt hat. Behind her, the two boys walk. Reuben first. He must be eight. Then Elisha, I think six. Leah, four, follows; and Sarah, two, walks hand in hand with my father. For a moment, I experience a pang, trying to recall if my father ever held my hand like that.

Batsheva comes up the porch stairs. She looks straight ahead, pretends she hasn't seen Christina and me. I am paralyzed, the way I am now in the streets of Jerusalem. Then Reuben passes. Then Elisha. And for some reason, it is Elisha—who years later will devote his life to studying Talmud and teaching—I remember most. He reaches no higher than my waist, just a boy, but his look of disapproval for our traveling on the holy day is so extreme, even as he pretends we do not exist. I have never been able to forget it.

After the others trail into the house, my father lingers with us on the porch. "It's the Sabbath," he says sheepishly. His face shows his displeasure and shame before he, too, averts his gaze.

"Let's go get you a cab." He opens the front door, then beckons us immediately into the basement.

I think I laughed, then, tromping down the basement stairs. "Wow, we can't even come in the living room. Nice, Dad. What's Christina gonna think of Orthodox Jews? Least we won't confuse it with Christianity, huh?" I don't remember my father answering. He made the call. And we left, with the rich smell of *cholent*, the traditional Sabbath meat-bean-and-barley stew, following us out to the street.

Years later, my father shares a saying: The cholent is "gerotn ins gast," meaning, the cholent is only as good as the guests. Meaning, if we heathens had eaten of the cholent, the meal would've been ruined. Corrupted. This is what Batsheva told my father that day in Teaneck when my friend and I interrupted their Sabbath. I also learned from my father that he considers this moment in his marriage one of the lowest points. Her treatment of me, and by turn, his, was shameful.

I wish my father could've stood up to his wife. Admonished his children. Something. We both might've felt some small relief. I regret my barbed humor, as well as forgetting it was the Sabbath. Looking back, I see so clearly how my father and I were both weak. Trapped by our own flaws and fears, troubled by the comforting scent of cooking cholent that seemed always just out of reach.

I return to the King David Hotel. To the large room I share with my father. I figure I don't have the right to complain, even though I am horribly uncomfortable sharing this intimate space. Yes, he is my father, but something . . . makes me shy.

We sit on opposite beds and talk.

"I went to the Old City," I say, telling him about the narrow streets, the bazaars, the old women who threatened to throw oranges at me. I talk about the mixing of Christian, Jewish, and Muslim cultures, the excitement, the golden light.

Then, I tell him about the religious man.

"He crab-walked down the wall, Dad. Like I was a disease."

My father looks disgusted. "What'd you expect?" he says with venom. "You chose to wear shorts." He walks out onto the balcony.

I want to scream, I didn't know!

But I can't get the words out.

I have trouble sleeping that night. I am constantly aware of my father's presence—his ragged breath, his bed creaking when he turns.

The next day, my father says more calmly, "You see, Rachel. You're young, attractive, and people respond. They're either interested or uncomfortable."

I flinch. I remember Batsheva's accusations of incest and inappropriateness. I remember the Lolita postcard my father sent when I graduated from college. I remember the appreciative looks he gave me when I came out of dressing rooms at Macy's with new school clothes, and the way those looks made me feel proud and pleased, but also uneasy.

"If you stay with your mother, if you choose to stay with her, Rachel, I will have to cut off all contact with you."

I am in seventh grade. I am already living with a friend of the family's because my mother can't take care of me anymore. So I am not in the best position to argue that I stay with my mother. But I hold off responding to my father's ultimatum for some months. Then, when the custody case goes to trial, I do it. I say to the judge, "I want to go with my father."

This was a turning point. I think something vital snapped in me then. After this, I hardened my heart. I loved my mother fiercely and didn't want to leave her. But the truth was, as my father pointed out, she had already left me.

I do not remember if my mother cried at the custody trial, if she was even there at all.

My brother goes with his blood relatives on his father's side, to Delaware.

I go with my father to New Jersey. He drives me in a rented U-Haul, even though I don't have enough belongings to even fill the floor of the truck. In the front, my Siamese cat Chocolate Chip prowls the seat, howling and clawing at my father's shoulders. My father barely says anything. In this way, looking back, I think he was doing his best.

Once, when I was in second grade and living in Alphabet City in Manhattan, my father came for a visit. He was petrified of the neighborhood. We were on the street, and a man came walking up with a pit bull on a thick chain. The dog growled and lunged at us. My father grabbed me by the shoulders and positioned me in front of him. I remember the dog's yellow eyes, the spit dripping from its mouth, the snapping of its jaws. But I wasn't scared. "I wasn't afraid!" I bragged to my father.

It is only years later that this memory returns. With it comes a dawning insight into my father's terrible weakness, and the fear underlying my childhood bravado.

After my father wins custody, we arrive in New Jersey.

My father doesn't take me home with him.

First I live with his adopted sister, Bett Rose. She has just divorced her husband, and kicked both him and her son out of the house. Bett and her daughter remain. We don't get off to a good start. "Before we do anything, your cat needs to be declawed," she says to me. When Chocolate Chip disappears into the woods and doesn't come back, I am sure she's been eaten by a dog because she couldn't defend herself. This doesn't help. Bett and her daughter enjoy lounging in bed all day, eating cake, watching TV. Me, I like to go in the big backyard, down to the Rahway River. Canoe, swim. Or climb out the bedroom window, onto the roof, and into the attic to shoot pool after Bett tells me it's off-limits. After a few months, my aunt kicks me out. "She's manipulative," she says to my father by way of explanation.

I tell my friend Margaret Solimine, who lives next door to Bett, about my plight. Margaret in turn tells her mother, who speaks with my father, who agrees to pay for my room and board at Margaret's house. I think maybe other kids won't notice the embarrassing fact that I've already moved in the first few months of living in Cranford, New Jersey.

This is the first time I don't have my own room. I share one with Kathleen, Margaret's older sister, because she has the bigger room with two twin beds. Kathleen is obsessed with rock stars, in particular Elton John. There are posters of him and other bands everywhere, and every day Kathleen wears another wacky pair of sunglasses to show her love. She is always playing records. It's the first time I hear Zeppelin. *Houses of the*

Holy. Upstairs on the third floor live the two older brothers, Mark and Josh. They have long shaggy hair and look like the rock stars in Kathleen's posters, except they're not as clean. Margaret tells me secretly they are juvenile delinquents. One sells pot, the other steals car parts. There is also the grandmother, a spry, compact woman. It's her house. She mostly keeps to herself, tucked away in a small sunny room on the second floor reading Church of Religious Science pamphlets. For fun, Margaret and I hide high up in the trees lining the street and throw pinecones at people's cars. We never get tired of the people stopping their cars, cursing, looking around for who might've lobbed the cones. Living here is not so bad.

But Margaret's mother, who is a chain-smoker and doesn't seem to have a job, keeps asking for more and more money, always with a new reason, until my father gets fed up. Time to move again.

So I stay with him for a few awkward days in Teaneck, while Batsheva is in the hospital giving birth to a third child.

Until one day, the phone rings. My father picks up.

"Thank you for your concern about Rachel."

"Who is it?" I whisper.

"Yes, Mrs. Haag. That's incredibly generous of you, Mrs. Haag."

Meanwhile, I'm waving my hands to get my dad's attention and shaking my head no, no, no. When that doesn't work, I try to grab the phone away.

"I will move her in this weekend," he says, and hangs up.

"Dad!"

He says nothing, but he looks pained.

"Mrs. Haag is my gym teacher! Everybody hates her!"

Mrs. Haag is horrible. Mrs. Haag is tone-deaf when she sings school songs, she has a shock of short orange hair, and she screams at everyone.

My life is over.

I don't tell anyone where I live. I let them think I still live where I was before. If I want to see my friends, I climb out the window and sneak away. I never invite them over, though sometimes I'll play Ping-Pong with Mr. Haag down in the basement.

When Mrs. Haag drives me to school and I see someone I know, I pretend I've dropped something on the floor of the car and duck my head down. Looking back, I have to hand it to Mrs. Haag for not calling me on that.

She calls me on a lot of other things though. As soon as I get home from school, she sends me out in the backyard with my field hockey stick to do drills. I think she wants to make me into an Olympic athlete. Maybe she's sad because her two sons are off at college and she can't tell them what to do anymore.

Mrs. Haag likes lists. She writes down chores for me to do and is surprised when I tell her I don't know how to do any of them. Including laundry.

"Well, maybe it's time you learned, young lady."

Another thing she says: "Rachel, I want you to see a therapist."

"Why? I'm fine."

"There's no way you can be fine with your background. I'm going to call your father. He doesn't know how to raise you."

I don't think my father appreciates that Mrs. Haag tries to boss him around and questions his parenting skills. After all, she's being paid to keep me.

One day, when we are eating salad from the deli, my father suddenly appears at the Haags'.

"Let's go, Rachel. You're leaving. Pack all your things."

"Mr. Resnick," says Mrs. Haag. "Hold on."

My father ignores her.

"How about I finish my dinner first, Dad. Is that okay?" I'm trying to joke. But no one seems to think this is funny. I burst into nervous laughter.

I go back to Teaneck with my father. Batsheva is furious and says this won't work.

Now he's really desperate.

One day I go to school and a kid taps me on the shoulder, shows me the local paper. "Is this you?" the kid says, pointing at a want ad for a boarding situation for a fourteen-year-old girl. "Yeah," I say nonchalantly. Even though I didn't know about the ad.

The Greens answer the ad. There's a mother who bakes Wesson oil cakes, a father who works in metallurgy, five kids—only two still home. They go to church, they make meat pasties and meals in Crock-Pots, they do arts and crafts, they wash their windows and put dust ruffles on their beds. They're what I think of as all-American. Finally. I don't really get them, but I think living with them will be good for me.

At the end of ninth grade, Mr. Green gets a job transfer to a small town in Alabama. I panic. I've only lived in Cranford for two and a half years. I can't move again.

My father offers me a choice.

"You can have your own apartment. I can set you up here in Cranford. Right near the high school. Or you can move with the Greens to Alabama."

"Dad, I'm only fifteen."

I decide to move to Alabama.

Looking back, I believe living with all these other families taught me a certain kind of resilience. Also adaptability. I always carried my personality with me. I think it was forged from brushing up against all those families.

When I bounced from one home to another, I realized pretty quickly that no matter how friendly people were, the truth is they were being paid to keep me. I was a job. It wasn't about love. Or family. I got the feeling that I was a burr in the hide of each family—in the sense that I had my own values, and they often clashed with the family's. Sometimes I felt my very existence was an affront. An offense. Calling into question the way they ordered their lives, goals, hopes, and dreams.

For years, it left me starving for love. And it made me very angry.

Still, I think what saved me as much as I am saved was not living with my mother or my father any longer than I did.

For this I am grateful.

On the night of my father's fiftieth birthday, we go to the Blue Note in Jerusalem to hear Stanley Jordan and Max Roach throw down some jazz. Afterward, my father says Max Roach was incredible.

I say, "I liked Jordan too."

"He was okay. I don't think he'll go too far."

I argue with my father, defend Jordan.

What were we fighting about? It couldn't have been jazz.

During middle school in Cranford, New Jersey, before I move to Alabama, my father comes to see me play field hockey. Batsheva and the kids are out of town, so he is able for once to see a Saturday game. I can't wait for him to watch me. I'm just a freshman but already a center half on the junior varsity team.

Afterward, I stand there in my kilt and cleats. Bruises cover my shins. I feel tall, proud, and strong. I ask him, "How was I?"

"You were good," he says. I smile.

"But Sonja Bergland, she was great."

Sonja Bergland. A redheaded state champion sprinter, also on the J.V. team as a freshman. Fleet of foot, a forward wing. Not his daughter. She is great, and I am merely good.

If love and sex addiction is passed down through the generations, like any other soul sickness, does this incident not connect to things like the following exchange?

My father, age sixty-six, at the kitchen table with his father, ninety-eight, eating. My father works on a bowl of ice cream. My grandfather cuts slices off a toffee bar. A serious sweet tooth runs in the family. No sentiment. But a sweet tooth.

"I was rereading *Hamlet*," my father says. "You know that part, where . . . I'm talking about Shakespeare. Dad? I thought you'd be interested."

His father pops a big piece of toffee into his mouth. Smiles broadly. Makes a mock grimace. "Shakespeare. Who needs him!" And he winks.

He winks, my father blinks.

Then my father tries to recover and smile, like he doesn't care, but he clearly does.

The grandfather, the moneymaker. The father, a lifelong student of literature and the Talmud, putting his faith in words, instead of wages.

He, like my mother, kept trying to get love from family.

But they had no love to give.

Downstairs in the King David Hotel lobby, we run into an old classmate of my father's from the yeshiva in New York.

"Hank Resnick!" she calls out. "Is this your wife?"

My father chuckles delightedly. Says nothing.

"No, I'm not!" I say hastily. "I'm his daughter."

"Well!" she says. "Do you know, in high school? Your father was a god. He played basketball, he was a scholar. If Hank Resnick said hi to you . . . He was a god."

Over and over on this two-week trip, my father vacillates between treating me like a wife—likely why sharing those small hotel rooms made my skin crawl—and letting me know I was not fully loved.

When we visit a kibbutz outside Tel Aviv, a man poses a question, one they ask all the parents in the kibbutz.

"Say you are on a bus with your child. And terrorists stop this bus. You are given a choice: You can save your child, or you can save yourself. Not both. Which would you choose?"

My father answers readily, "Well, I would save myself." And he smiles.

I smile too. A smile of stupidity, and shock, and wanting to seem agreeable.

He's made me feel this way before—shut out, unloved, alone.

It was the summer of 1981. I was eighteen, about to enroll at Yale that fall. I was visiting my father in New Jersey, where I'd planned to reconnect and stay until school started. Because I was not welcome at his house, where his wife and four children from his second marriage lived, I stayed at his parents' house. I sat on the Posturepedic bed in the guest room while my father sat stiffly in a Victorian chair. Every surface displayed needle-point: pillows, pictures my grandmother had stitched and framed. A family tree with my name embroidered onto a branch with different thread than the other names.

"Why can't we spend more time together, Dad? I've barely seen you."

"I have four young children, Rachel."

"I'm your child."

No answer.

"Are you okay, Dad?" I say anxiously. "Do you feel all right?"

"Not really."

Something drops inside. A question forms without any connection to my brain.

"Dad?" I say tentatively. He doesn't answer. Bows his head in his hands.

"Are you even happy I'm here? I mean, I get the feeling . . . you don't even like me or something." I'm being dramatic. I assume he'll rush in with reassurance.

He lifts his head then. Looks at me directly. "You want the truth? Truth is, Rachel. I love you. And I hate you."

In my memory of that day, everything goes blank after that.

One morning in Tel Aviv, in an effort to learn some Judaica, I ask my father about child sacrifice. Abraham, Isaac. Molech, whom he often mentions. "What's it really about?" Looking back, I think I was baiting him.

My father puts down his forkful of herring. "It's really about discomfort with death," he says. "Not wanting to die. A bid for immortality. When you sacrifice a child, you are sacrificing youth. It's a generational conflict." He takes a bite of herring. "It's about killing your own child so you don't have to die."

Toward the end of the trip, in the gorgeous town of Galilee with the magical glassy water, the biblical depths, the pastel light, I ask a question I have always wanted to ask but never dared. Emboldened by the trip, the time spent together, I finally do.

"Dad, did you love Jane?"

We are sitting at a restaurant overlooking the Sea of Galilee. My father picks at his fish, separates out a few bones before taking a bite. He's wearing a floppy white tennis hat low over his face.

"No."

I close my eyes for a second. "I mean, you know, at some point? In the beginning? Like, maybe when you met in that Shakespeare class at Columbia, and she was wearing a sweatsuit way before anyone wore them? Or when you guys . . ." I trail off.

"I never loved your mother." My father's voice isn't angry, exactly. It has an edge. There is also a weariness, and a tinge of sadness. Still, it was brutal.

I never loved your mother.

I love you and I hate you.

I would save myself.

These sentiments unleashed—not then, not yet, but in months and years to come—a typhoon of anger that I think drove me deeper into the arms of undesirable, dangerous men. Over and over, I reenacted the withdrawal of a man's love, as taught to me by both parents. Until I hit a wall. I would have to scale that wall, bricked with the broken headstones of my father, his father, his father's father, my mother, her mother, her mother's mother, or lose my chance to find sustaining love.

Four months after our historic trip to Israel, my father asks me to do him a favor.

"How's your sanity," he says by way of an opening gambit. Knowing I am concerned about it. Knowing my mother's history.

Then he tells me he's going to meet Noga in Israel. Noga is his new girlfriend. Noga, whom he speaks about in sugared tones when we chat, in a way that makes my neck hair bristle. They met in the library where he works.

"I'm going to tell my boss I'm visiting you in California," he says.

It's not really a question. Still, I say okay at first. Then I say, "You know, I don't feel comfortable with that. I don't want to be implicated."

And he says, "You won't forget this." His tone is nasty. It wouldn't have surprised me if he never spoke to me again. He has that capacity. Still, I stand my ground. His final coup de grace? Well then, he will just have to withdraw his promised support of paying for my graduate writing degree.

This is nothing new.

In 1995, four years later, my father sends me an old laptop of his to use.

When I open it up, I see that his diaries and other personal writings are still on the computer.

I stare, dumbfounded. I struggle against the impulse to open the files.

Part of me thinks he left them there for me to read.

The other part of me simply can't resist the thought of reading them whether he meant me to or not.

Still, I don't read them for some weeks.

When I do finally click open the diaries, I feel like a fist comes right out of the computer screen and punches me in the mouth.

I also feel a surge of compassion.

What I learn from reading his diaries is that he is a sex addict, his marriage sucked, and that he did not feel loved as a husband, or as a child.

I divide men into two rough categories: those who remind me of my father, and those who remind me of my brother.

Those who remind me of my father tend to be the ones I fall in love with—the dangerous ones. The ones who can't commit, who abandon, who betray. Of course they arrive in charming, gifted packages.

Those who remind me of my brother fill me with sisterly love, a protectiveness, an urge to tease, a deep and abiding affection.

When Michael was three, and I was eleven, he went to live with his father's family. My brother and I have only kept in spotty touch for years, until I graduate from college, move to Los Angeles, and decide to rescue him. I want to remove him from what I consider a detrimental environment. I want to save him, send him to college. He becomes my special project.

I start by ordering catalogs from every single college I deem suitable. I set up a guest room for my brother. Find him temporary jobs. Research cars.

Then, I fly back East, pick up a drive-away car that needs to be driven back West, and pick him up in Delaware. Although he's agreed to the adventure, he comes reluctantly. Gone is the short, towheaded, mischievous boy I remembered so well. In his stead is a somber man-boy of six foot four, with the armspan of an orangutan. He's formidable, brooding. He's dressed in punk style, with a scarf festooned with skulls, his size-fourteen Doc Martens, and a gloomy attitude to match. On occasions his razor wit emerges. That is, when he isn't suffering from depression.

The plan is we will both drive.

But after the first few minutes with Michael at the wheel—when he jumps the median divider on the highway, even after taking NoDoz—I decide I will drive the whole way. And I do.

On that drive, round about the New Mexico border when the desert air is blowing in the side windows, my brother begins to groan. He ducks his head into his arms, and presses his temples, and groans some more.

"What's wrong with you? That truck stop chicken 'n' gravy go to your head?"

"I have a tumor."

"What?"

"I have a brain tumor, Rachel. I can feel it."

I wrinkle my brow, catch a glimpse of my brother out of the corner of my eye. "If this is 'cuz you think I'm going to make you drive, don't worry."

"I HAVE A BRAIN TUMOR!" my brother bellows.

Without thinking, I scratch my neck and almost plow into a green Gremlin.

"Michael . . ." He is silent. I think, though I'm not sure, that this is about something else. "Is there anything I can do? You want me to call a doctor? Want some aspirin? A burger?"

Michael sits up suddenly, stares bug-eyed at the highway streaming by. Then, after about three crappy songs play on the radio, he turns to look at me.

"I'm just a big fat brain," he says. "That is all I am."

In L.A., I set Michael up with a futon. I pile the college catalogs nearby. I show him the *L.A. Weekly*. I talk about places to go, people to see, meet, things to do. But my brother is listless. My brother spreads the linens on the futon and sits, cross-legged, and does not move. He is like a man-boy version of the hookah-smoking caterpillar in *Alice in Wonderland*, except he is not smoking a hookah, and he is more fleshy than a caterpillar. Still, he sits there like that, with a kind of dazed and solid calmness.

One day I convince him to go for a drive on his own. He gets about fifteen minutes away, then returns. Shaken. Pale.

"I can't do it, Rachel. I can't. The cars. I don't know. I can't do it." And he throws the keys down on the hardwood floor and sits on the futon.

He will not read the catalogs. He will not apply. Hell, he won't even discuss college. I can't interest him in meeting with special-effects guys from film, or any other possible gigs.

After a couple of weeks of this, I realize, it's only a matter of time. I lost my brother once, when he was three. I am going to lose him again.

Even if it seems crazy, I feel guilty. Granted I was only eleven when our mother lost custody. What could I have done to keep my brother and me together? To take care of him? Now is my chance to make things right.

Which is why I am sickened to consider that possibly I was at fault during this Los Angeles rescue mission. That I failed in not being able to handle him. That I had a chance, and I drove my brother away.

One night, I cook dinner. An attempt at Cuban fare, with white rice and black beans, and fried plantains. Before we even get a chance to eat, Michael clumsily knocks the plate with his elbow and it smashes in two on the floor. Michael leaps up, tries to gather the shards with his hands, flustered, muttering apologies, his huge body hunched—and I do not say, "It's okay. Don't worry." I say, "Don't touch it! Let me get that. Just sit down! Jesus!"

It is the first time I've lost my temper in these weeks. Michael sits, and it is like he transforms into a human explosive. His jaw sets, clenches. His eyes darken from blue to black. His face flushes red. I swear I can see steam coming out of his ears. Fists clenched, body tensed and looking as if he'll lift off.

"Michael, I'm sorry . . ." I say, terrified. Mortified. Full of regret. But it is too late. The color in his face rises even more. Now I am scared. Michael is a very big boy.

"You had it worse than me, Michael. I'm so sorry. You get all the slack in the world. I'm so sorry. I forgot. You had it so much worse . . ."

Michael stands suddenly, heaves the table back. He is shockingly strong. It slides across the room, this heavy marble bistro table. Then he swipes his hand onto the table and takes up two huge handfuls of plantains, and smears them all over his face. Saying nothing.

I stand stock-still. Then I back slowly away to the other side of the room. Near the phone. In case I have to call 911.

"You happy now? Dear sister? You happy now? Huh? Huh? Huh?"

He lurches toward me, his face wild, plantains smearing his cheeks, his forehead, sliding down his Irish-English face, the broad planes, the angry mouth.

"Calm down," I say, quietly. It is like facing off with a grizzly. It is like trying to talk sense to an electrical storm. I don't move a muscle.

"Let me get you a towel," I say, when I see he's cooling off.

I walk slowly, deliberately, to the bathroom.

The spell is broken.

When I return, Michael is sitting bent over at the table. He seems to have shrunk.

"I should go back to Delaware," he says. "I didn't want to tell you. I don't like it here. I don't want to go to college. Okay? Okay? Okay? I want to go home."

And so, we book a ticket. And he goes.

I scarcely see my brother as time goes on.

One day I realize ten years have passed since we last saw each other. And he only lives in Austin, Texas. Not so far from Los Angeles. I also haven't spoken with my father in six months. A total of two years will pass before I reconnect with him.

How Michael ultimately got returned to me, and then how my father also was returned to me, is all completely and utterly thanks to the awareness that I am a love junkie. Thanks to my walking into the rooms of a twelve-step support group for other people who are love junkies. Where I finally find a place where I belong. A place that began to help me heal and make sense of this sabra—peel back the thorny shell and find what was sweet within. It was time to become human.

It was time to grow up.

CHAPTER SEVEN

Hitting Bottom

2004

We are at Hump, a restaurant situated high above the Santa Monica airport runway. Outside, small planes descend into a night pricked by red landing lights. Spencer and I are engaged in extreme eating, which includes things like cockscombs, bone marrow, and sheep's heads. Here at Hump the emphasis is on sushi. Most of the menu is fresh-killed. I don't want to be here. But I'll do anything to keep this relationship alive.

"Live product makes for better eating," says Spencer. He runs a meaty hand over his shaved head. His mother named him after Spencer Tracy because she had a mad crush on him back in Poland. No Jerzy or Czeslaw for him.

I drink the snapping-turtle-blood cocktail and try to smile.

As the viscous liquid slides slowly down my throat, an involuntary shudder courses through my body. I gaze outside to regain my composure. The landing lights whisper danger, and the dark makes a swooping sound that only I can hear. If I

173

turn my fork just so, place my napkin with point draped precisely between my thighs, if I ignore the swoops and whispers, I will make it all fine. I will convince him I am the woman he wants.

Spencer wipes his lips; a crimson drop still stains the corner of his mouth.

I remember Eddie, gorging on lamb-face meat stuffed into a cone of newspaper. We were seated at a food stall smack in the middle of the famous square of Djemma el-Fna in Marrakesh. I said something to get his attention, I don't know what. When Eddie turned to me, a bit of brain clung to his lip. It glistened there, like a maggot.

"I've got a joke," says Spencer. "What makes a strawberry milkshake?"

"No idea."

"When a man punches a woman in the mouth then comes on her face."

I'm silent. "That's not funny," I say. But I don't move. If I get up, if I tell him his joke's warped and juvenile, that his humor disturbs me, he might leave. Please don't leave me. I can't take another one leaving.

A memory whooshes in: I am three or four years old. I am in the bathtub in the apartment on West 110th Street, playing with these colorful plastic bath toys. You snap them together, make a big necklace, and they float around. But now I'm bored. The water's cold. My fingertips are all pruny. I've been in here a long time. "Ma," I call out. I plunge the toys under the water, and they bounce right back up. I hate being cold. I pull the toys apart, put them back together, a bunch of times. After a while,

I start shouting. "Ma? Ma! Ma! Maaaaaaaaaa!" The shouting warms me up. I splash the walls, throw bath toys on the floor, continue yelling. I remember being mad. But when I think about it now, was it anger? What would a four-year-old kid who's left alone, unattended, in a bathtub, really feel?

Spencer's voice brings me back.

"Aw, jeez. Lighten up! Where's that brassy anything-goes girl I know? The one whose online profile mentioned loving *Baise-Moi* and *Betty Blue*?"

I met Spencer a month ago. I found him on Nerve.com. He was fresh out of a long-term relationship, and on paper, seemed almost too good to be true. I wanted to snatch him before anyone else got a chance. "It's like I cooked you up somehow," I wrote in that first giddy e-mail. Almost ten years had passed since Eddie, ten years and a long line of one-night stands, short-term relationships, and relationships-in-my-head like Winchester. I am still unmarried, still single, still broke, still yearning. This is not how it was supposed to go. I want to squirm right out of my life. When Spencer and I met, I knew he was the one. I latched onto him like he was a human respirator and I was gasping for my last breath.

"The chef cuts the throat of the turtle while he's still alive," says Spencer.

I hold back a gag reflex. I am an accomplice in murder. The heavy liquid sloshes inside me. I wish I could open a door in my stomach and let the offending drink drain out.

I didn't want to come tonight. Two weeks ago, this man impregnated me. He took it for granted that I was using contraception, and I let him think so, distracting him with hungry kisses and impassioned blow jobs. I know he's used steroids—stackers; Equipoise, the horse steroid, self-injected into his buttocks; double doses of Deca; Winstrol cycles . . . never mind. He told me he has supersperm, and at my age, that's paramount. I will just try to cut down other pregnancy risks, and pray. "You're not supposed to eat raw fish," I had said earlier in Spencer's funky Venice Beach bungalow. "It can cause problems. I'm forty-one." I tried to keep the edge out of my voice, but like a saw, it bit through the fabric of my words. "If the kid's deformed, we can blame it on this meal," Spencer had said. "Stop worrying." The reservations had already been made and Spencer thought I was being silly.

We are going to be a family soon—father, mother, and baby. So it's time to buck up. Rein in the sensitivity and forget the racing heart. We will stick together no matter what, because that is what families are supposed to do.

I realize now what that four-year-old kid in the bathtub must've felt, underneath the rage: pure terror.

A Cessna glides past outside the dark windows. I concentrate on the fullness I feel, the way being pregnant gives me power. I can grow things inside me. I even dream fertile: Thick vines explode from pots, climb, grasp, push through walls. At last, I am rooted. Just try to knock me over. You haven't met stubborn until you've met me. I will be one hell of a mother.

Spencer notes my reluctance to partake. I was hoping one sip would've sufficed.

"In most primitive cultures, blood from a freshly slaughtered animal is customarily offered to VIPs. Drink up, doll."

I love this man. He is so knowledgeable. So articulate. He is everything I've ever wanted.

"Shall we drink?" I say, ignoring my misgivings about the ill effects on a pregnancy.

We clink glasses.

"A toast. To Ajax, whose time has come." I stiffen, say nothing. "The bird's got to go, Rachel," says Spencer. "You know a homicidal parrot in the same house as a baby . . ."

I drain my glass, consider his point, though the attachment is intense. The bird's been there through a host of men. How could I abandon him? The thought of Ajax bouncing from home to home makes me sick.

"I will think about it," I say. "I know you're right."

Spencer shakes his head in disgust. Just like my father.

I reach across the table and grasp Spencer's big-knuckled hand. "I'm so happy you're going to be the father of my child." I stroke his fingers. "I feel so lucky."

"I told you," he said, "I've got some kind of supersperm. I can get a rock pregnant."

Spencer is special. If you take a mold of the roof of his mouth, you will see there an exact replica of the profile of Abraham Lincoln. "I have proof at my dentist's in Beverly Hills," he says. Spencer told me he has a two-inch patch of skin on his right forearm from which emanates the sweetest, most exotic perfume. I try to smell it, but am not able to detect anything. Since Spencer has an odd sense of humor and studied semiotics, I am never sure if he is kidding. Maybe he has a more highly developed sense of smell than I. Certainly his tastes are unusual. He owns his own personal bone marrow spoon. He especially loves the smell of skunk.

The following week, we are in my home in Topanga Canyon. Ajax is on my shoulder. Spencer moves toward me. Ajax leans down and seizes my ear. "Fuck," I say. You cannot hit a bird, because they are too fragile. Their necks are thin and might snap. All their strength is concentrated in their beaks. Plus, hitting makes them even more aggressive. I shake Ajax from my shoulder. On the floor, Ajax sprints toward Spencer's leg with the intention to drill his foot. Spencer retreats to the bedroom, closes the door. Blood spurts from my ear.

I found Ajax through a bird rescue service. I drove six hours north to Gilroy, the Garlic Capital of the World, to pick up Ajax from his interim caretaker. We met in a Denny's parking lot. I'd specifically requested no abused pets, knowing how much more trouble they were. The rescue service assured me Ajax was well loved. But when I met him, the surrogate who'd been keeping him told me he'd been abused for his first three years. By that point, it was too late. I was in love with this Technicolor creature with his azure blue, jungle green, and scarlet feathers, his flashing eyes and awe-inspiring beak. I took him home. On the way, he vomited in my lap, which for birds is a sign of affection. They are trying to feed the one they love.

The pain in my ear is sharp. I reach up, feel something like a tiny twig on my lobe. Already I have scars on my chest, back, calf, and forearms. Dizzy, I grab a towel and edge slowly toward the bird, drop the towel over his body and flip him, binding his beak to prevent any more stabbing.

After I wrestle the bird into a towel and then into his cage, Spencer tends to my ear. Removes something. The pain is startling. The bird growls from the cage. He wants Spencer gone. Parrots often bond with one person. Ajax thinks Spencer is a cuckold. I am ashamed to say, some sick part of me might enjoy two creatures fighting for my affections.

"Cartilage," he says, "does not grow back. Your ear is going to be permanently deformed."

I remember the sound of my mother's footsteps. She'd broken an ankle years ago and never gotten it fixed. When she walked, she stepped normally with one foot, then walked on tippy-toe with the other. The irregular footfalls drove me nuts. Step, swish, step, swish. Like I was supposed to feel sorry for her. Every time she got on her feet.

Because my mother was crazy, does that mean I am crazy too? Does it mean my brain is deformed?

Only looking back do I realize these questions, questions that have floated in and out of my consciousness for decades, are some of the driving forces behind looking for that fix. That all-encompassing, all-consuming love drug. Anything to avoid facing questions I prefer to leave unanswered.

I found Spencer at just the right moment. After years spent trying to find a soul mate, then switching my fanatic pursuit to a sperm donor, and failing on both counts, I was through. Or so I thought. Until one day I trolled online and saw Spencer. The perfect victim to make my dreams come true.

*   *   *

It is 2000, four years before I meet Spencer, the dawn of the twenty-first century. I am thirty-seven. I am desperate.

Where is my daughter? I can see her so clearly. Can feel her baby-fine hair in my hands as I comb through the strands, feel the sweet weight of her on my lap. Can see her eyes flutter closed as I sing "Swing Low, Sweet Chariot" or "Down in the Valley"—wait, those are songs my mother once sang to me, once upon a time, with her rich contralto, when we lived on West 110th Street, when she sang me to sleep in that pretty white-painted bed. I can still see her shadow in the doorway, feel her sit on the mattress so it sags toward her. I can feel how she held me in her arms, stroked my hair, leaned in close enough so I could feel her breath skein over my sleepy face before I drifted off. Or at least that is how I remember it.

The desire to have my own daughter draws me so powerfully that I think it must be ordained. I think I am responsible for forcing it to happen.

I can't help myself. As the anxiety grows with the passing years, I propose fatherhood to a handful of inappropriate men.

The first one I ask is Knute, the sexy, six-foot-three screenwriter from South Boston with Russian mob connections and a passion for drink. He likes to insult me. One night, I dared him to kiss me at a party, and he did. It was one of those electric kisses. It left me weak in the knees and half mad.

That night, we slept together. Sort of. "I don't usually have these problems," he said. "Usually I can go all night. Normally." Then he fell asleep. The next morning he said, very quietly, as I was standing naked, "You look like a goddess." Or, I think he did.

Maybe I just want him to have said that. I know later that same morning he said, "I hate that hat you're wearing."

I thought we were in love. He just didn't know how to say it. I thought he would arrive at my doorstep on Valentine's Day bearing flowers, presents, declarations of love. Instead, I didn't hear from him for months. And we never slept together again, though we are now friends.

When I ask him, when I e-mail my proposition, he is in Hungary directing his first film. A hired bear has just broken loose from the set. Knute has his hands full; he is also drinking so much vodka I imagine it replacing the blood in his veins. I worry what that might do to sperm.

It was an intense proposition. I guess I shouldn't have been surprised when he didn't respond.

I write him again, chiding him for not writing me. "What, I ask you to father a kid with me and you can't even write back?" I'm one dignified gal. Knute writes back right away and says he is sorry, he had written back. Maybe the e-mail got lost. "What I said was, I'm really flattered. And I thought about it. A lot. But the truth is, it's not the way I want to have a kid. I want to have one with someone I marry . . . So I'll have to pass."

Stung to the core, for a moment I wonder if I am manipulating him, using the idea of parenting to hook Knute back in. No matter. I return to my obsessive quest to have a baby. I am not so deflated by Knute's rejection that I will give up. Yet.

The second man I ask is Charles.

Charles is gay. Charles is the chief of the Williwak tribe. There are only three card-carrying members of the Williwak tribe left on the planet, and they elect Charles to be their chief.

He also knows all the lyrics to all Dolly Parton's songs. He is good-looking, my height, and seriously buff. Maybe too buff. I wonder whether he's used steroids, and whether that would affect sperm. Would the child be *born* buff, or lopsided in some way? This is before Spencer, before utter desperation.

We exchange some e-mails and bandy about the idea of being co-parents like it's some kind of charming game of badminton. Charles says he is seriously considering it.

When the prospect gets more real, when we speak of doctors, and inseminations, and visitation, however, we both balk. Until we lose touch completely.

The third man I ask is Petros. We were involved for three years, but he was unable to commit. When I ask him, he is living in Greece, married for a second time, and has a child of his own.

"Don't you want an American kid? You know, balance out your American side and your Greek side?"

Petros, ever polite, says he'll think about it. But he never responds directly to my queries and follow-ups. This is exactly how he let our relationship slip politely away.

After this, I am too ashamed to ask anyone else. I experience a hollowness that feels almost unbearable.

I give up.

One night, a few weeks after meeting Spencer, I return home from teaching and I find my bed strewn with rose petals.

The scent overwhelms me, and I fall to my knees and weep. How did I get so lucky? I lie naked in those petals, think of this man, whom I believe I've been waiting for all my life. I go into the bathroom to wash up and see scrawled on my bathroom mirror in bright pink lipstick: I LOVE YOU.

"I broke into your house," Spencer says when I call his cell phone. I can almost sense him grinning over the line. "I am the thief of your heart."

And it is not even Valentine's Day.

Wait. Was that how it happened? When I think back, when I take my time, I remember my initial reaction upon discovery of the break-in: panic. Why were there rose petals on my bed? What the fuck was going on? Did I give Spencer a key and forget? Was he here? Was someone else here? But the apartment was still, except for Ajax chewing food and dropping it into his water dish to make it moister.

If I slow down, if I try to re-create those early moments, at first sight it all made my flesh shiver. Thinking of Spencer rifling through my drawers, through my makeup, like he lived there, moving through my bedroom when I wasn't around, taking possession—how long had he stayed? What else had he touched? Why did he think this was okay?

I must've banished these feelings so fast and replaced them with rose-colored rationalizations: He was simply overcome by love; they were gestures of a grand passion! Not an unwanted intrusion, not an invasion of space, not a violation. I transformed the anxiety into warm romantic tingling and sexual excitation. I ignored any red flags.

This came back to haunt me when he broke in later with intention to hurt and destroy.

Still, I never did make Spencer a key to my home. Not the

whole time we were together. Perhaps that was a small sign of health, hiding deep within.

My mother carried files with her wherever she went. Manila folders stuffed into accordion-file organizers crammed into beat-up leather satchels. Folders with names of different family members. Inside, the folders held letters these family members had written. To Jane. About Jane. Along with many letters from lawyers. And doctors. The lawyers demanded her rights, the doctors testified to her mental health progress and physical well-being. And my mother herself wrote countless letters stating her position, pleading her case. My mother was always building a case. Especially after she lost custody of me and Michael. The world was against her. In particular, her family was out to get her. She was constantly trying to get their attention, and acknowledgment. Their approval. In return, she was treated as an outcast. A scapegoat. It is possible that there was truth in all her suspicions. It is also possible that there was a chemical condition, a mental predilection for paranoia and distorting that truth. I don't know. I do know many families have trouble handling those with mental illness. I do know sometimes families try to shut them out, pretend they don't exist, marginalize—perhaps even annihilate them. At least that is what Jane thought, as this excerpt from a letter she wrote six months before her untimely death at age thirty-six illustrates: "The unscrupulous use of my two children to punish and diminish me, to deprive me of purpose, of hope, and, to possibly destroy them, will not go unrecognized—my rights as a mother and as a human being have been denied."

My mother dramatically modeled how to be a world-class victim. I lapped up the lessons and swallowed the paranoia without the slightest awareness of what I was doing. So little sets it off. Even though I didn't say anything to Spencer after his romantic break-in, I realize now that was when I first became suspicious. This secret belief that people were ultimately out to get me would slowly seep into our relationship, and help to poison it completely.

One night, we go to the bowling alley. Before we part, Spencer buys me a carton of saltines for my truck, for my house, and for his bungalow. The crackers help keep the pregnancy nausea at bay.

"I'm afraid," I say to Spencer. "Hold me." I think about worried wombs, something mothers who are old enough to be grandmothers can feel. Am I one of those? Trying to stave off death? Who am I, to have a child naturally at this age? I want it so badly I can't think straight.

Spencer squints. "Jesus, Rachel. You know, when I first met you, I thought you were my brain in a pinup body. Now I just think you're Woody Allen with tits. You're so fucking neurotic."

When I tear up, he says, "Rachel, aren't you excited? We're having a baby. We're going to have a beautiful baby."

At six weeks and two days, I bleed. At first, I think the pale pink smudge on the toilet tissue is a lipstick trace. But the next morning after bowling, a single glistening bead of crimson spots the tissue. Then, two more peeings, and nothing. No blood. Maybe I'm safe.

At this point, the fertilized egg has gone through costume changes as zygote, morula, and blastocyst. Now it is an embryo, already suspended in amniotic fluid, no bigger than a hair follicle. Its fate in the balance.

I remember what Spencer said about the snapping-turtle-blood cocktail.

"Egg whites create a kind of emulsion, so the platelets are suspended in wine."

This baby is staying put. She is floating.

I go to the gyno.

The ultrasound shows a silent grainy womb, a small dot of light—that's the egg sac—and dark shadows cascading down the womb walls, toward the cervix.

The blood is pouring down.

Threatened AB is scrawled on the gynecologist's bill. A threatened spontaneous abortion.

There must be a way to hold this baby in my womb. Surely there is hope.

Chromosomal, they say. When it's this early, the body ejects what is not forming right. Nature, they say. You are forty-one. You are lucky you got pregnant.

The nurse, Jean, folds her arms around me. And I weep. How could this happen? A step away, months, from a home, a family, parenthood. Purpose.

I call Stasia, tell her the news, and she bursts into tears.

The following morning, I pass what looks like a miniature placenta with a tiny yellowish egg sac. I study it there in the toilet tissue, think about burying it. But maybe that is morbid. So tiny. This could develop into a baby? Before I can obsess, I flush it away. I can't stop weeping. I had never understood how wondrous it is, how truly miraculous. Babies.

The depression takes root. Digs in deep, replacing those leafy green vines with its dark shadows.

I still don't see how close I am to the bottom. Even though I am scraping it.

In 1971, my father bought me a one-year diary from Macy's. I didn't write in it much. The few pages that I filled are mostly about upsetting incidents, bad memories, complaints, and confessions. As if writing them down would make them go away. Or at least, bear witness. One memory starts like this: "When school was over Batsheva was waiting for me instead of Daddy." I fill in the blanks.

I'm sitting in the car with Batsheva. She is driving. We don't talk. We go through the Holland Tunnel and I hold my breath. Tonight was supposed to be a rare dinner with me and my father. "I think she came just so she could get all Daddy's attention to her instead of me." We arrive at my favorite diner, and for once, the aquamarine and orange colors don't make my heart leap. We slide into the booth. There's not much room for me. "It was true, because when I went to Howard Johnson's Daddy wanted to give attention to her and not me." Batsheva talks loud and fast. She tells my father something about Hebrew school, and a broken radiator hose. I sit there, quietly, watching my father, studying his face and expressions, but he doesn't even look at me, or barely, except when I fumble with the fries and spill ketchup on my shirt. Other times, when my father and I eat at the diner, we laugh and he tells stories, and we share pistachio ice cream. Now he looks sad and doesn't say much. It's like he forgot who I was. I want to disappear. In my diary, I write: "I think Daddy doesn't like me. Also he hasn't been very happy I think. I don't know why. Does he still love me? I don't know. It might be because I got his TV antenna broken or that I got some things on my clothes? I don't know."

Does he still love me?

I have been asking that same question now over and over for almost four decades. With every man I've known.

One night, frantic to move through my grief faster, speed up the mourning process so I don't lose Spencer, I find a pregnancy-loss bereavement group in Canoga Park. Spencer can't make it. I go alone.

The room is small, a private office crowded with chairs, eight people, and a volunteer therapist as our guide. The sadness is palpable. Dense. It's in the air, it's soaked into the carpets, it's sewn into the upholstery. Sadness is etched in the face of every person present. There is an eighty-seven-year-old woman still haunted by a stillborn baby she gave birth to half a century ago. There are couples who seem to stay upright only because they are leaning on each other, couples who can't seem to get pregnant, or stay pregnant, who visit their unborn children's graves every weekend bearing silent picnics, years after the miscarriages or stillbirths occurred. One husband says that after so many tries, and so many losses, he "can't stand the aggressive presence of babies everywhere."

When I speak, the group reassures me that what I'm feeling is normal. Such depression is to be expected. This quality of grief, common. I can't wait to go home and tell Spencer. To share what I've learned about the necessity of mutual mourning for couples, thinking I've pinpointed our problem. I vow never to go to this group again. I learned what I needed. Besides, I can't bear the weight of their grief.

What I don't realize then is the grief I felt crushing me was my own.

And I had carried it since childhood.

A week after the miscarriage, Spencer breaks up with me. I don't know how long I stand there in his bungalow, watching him lounging on the couch, avoiding my eyes, smoking Sobranie after Sobranie. Finally, I leave.

Not for long. After calling every friend, crying, tearing at my hair and clothes, driving aimlessly, I find myself at a florist. I buy the most magnificent bouquet of tiger lilies and wild ginger, a bird-of-paradise—and I find myself, just as mysteriously, back at Spencer's, only a few hours later. I use my key. I let myself in.

"I love you, Spencer," I say. Hand him the flowers. He smiles softly. Wraps me in his strong arms. And holds me, as I shake, and sob, and cling—as if my life depends on it.

And it does.

Because he is my life. My life before? Hardly a trace remains: I've lost touch with many friends, family; I've ignored work and myself. I am completely and utterly lost.

There is one chilling moment that sums this up: I am driving, and speed-dialing Spencer over and over on the cell phone, punching buttons with increasing frenzy, staring down at the instrument as if to will him to pick up. Desperate to reach him. Desperate to explain, to mend things after a fight. I am so desperate, so obsessed, I smash right into the rear end of a van. Right there, on the Hollywood Freeway, during rush hour.

We pull over to the side of the road, and I am horrified to see that the van holds a five-strong Korean family, including a frail-seeming grandfather and an infant—who was not strapped into a car seat.

An infant, who was not strapped into a car seat.

No matter that this is illegal; a child may be hurt. A human being under one year of age may be injured. And I am responsible.

She seems all right. Everyone seems all right. It's just a fender bender. We are all lucky—I am lucky, I am damn lucky—that the traffic was so thick and slow we were barely moving. But the baby is crying violently, inconsolably, and the mother tries to soothe her by placing her palm on the child's forehead. And the mother looks at me with hatred.

Looking back, I see that I could not let go of Spencer. If I did, I would've had to face the emptiness. And quite possibly my own insanity.

We get back together.

Over two evenings near Christmas, a tumultuous period a month before the end, I e-mail Spencer sixty-four times.

Throughout the relationship, I send no fewer than three e-mails a day, and once send thirty in a twenty-four-hour period.

"This meeting of ours is some kind of cosmic present." And on and on.

"It somehow feels like puzzle pieces are interlocking, all over the place, in this other dimension . . . The fusion of fantasy and reality is a heady one."

"You're making not only all of my past pale but now you're draining color from everyone else's . . . All my friends want to be your girlfriend!"

"Greedy girl, now wanting more and more of you . . . all this, flying in the face of a parade of disappointments, heart-aches, yearnings . . . Are you going to call me a damn bottomless well because I say that?"

If he had, he would've been right.

In a note to Petros, a few weeks after meeting Spencer, I say: "I met a man . . . followed on the heels of some of the lowest points of my life. Capped by a speeding ticket (almost four hundred dollars) and insurance poised to go sky-high . . . was in a state of 'can't win for losing' despair. Head-banging soul-searching what'm I doing wrong, sad, lonely—so tired of doing it all alone. Feeling like seven years in the desert. Then I meet this man."

I am aware enough to say, "Not everything is solved. He's very similar to me in many ways, including being not money-focused and super-solvent. But he adores me, and brings happiness. And that not being alone . . ."

Depleted. Soul-sick. Seeking someone to rescue. Seeking someone to fix.

I am a victim—of myself.

Later, when things fall apart, the relationship dies a thousand deaths—every single time I go back for more. Determined to

191

make it happen. To force it. I am like a zombie, the undead, a bounce-back punching bag. Nothing keeps me down. Or away.

The sixty-four e-mails are alternately berating and blaming, then apologetic and pleading. They are uniformly pathetic. And indicate a severe depression I would not admit.

"I have such a feeling of dread when I am not ready to give up—and still have hope. Do you? . . . I'm really shaken now."

"Just wish I could fuck you. I'd like you to think of me in thigh-high stockings, or fishnets, or silk ones with garters, your pleasure, and spiky heels, and pleated skirt, and white buttoned-down shirt, tapping away at a keyboard perched in a chair."

"I want this to work so much it's triggered my insecurities and some darkness with fear of loss . . . I will try very hard to listen better."

"Very very sorry my e-mails were overwhelming and off-putting. Very sorry about that. Seems I can't do it right—so sorry."

Spencer sees my behavior as "an ocean of negative, then a ray of pure, beautiful sunshine, then gloom. And on and on as a loop."

He also sees this: "The enormous divide between what you say in e-mails (sweet flowery promising all kind of affection and attention) and the reality of when you show up, monotone, complaining about your life, following through on nothing—gets no attention from you."

I completely compromise, discard even the fantasy. Anything to keep a shred of a connection. Even though nothing's working anymore. There's no pleasure left in this game.

I write, "Much as I wanted to swoon into the big things, marriage, ring, surprise engagement party, moving in—the truth is none happened." Then I choose to let go of the three times he'd proposed to me, however halfheartedly or haphazardly. I dismiss all the other broken promises, too. I add, "Okay, forget ring, marriage, trips, my fantasy of a subsidized life. That's all totally out of the picture."

And unbelievably, up to the bitter end, when Spencer finally acts in a sane way and cuts things off for good, I still say this: "Isn't there a way we can try to start fresh?"

I am seated on Spencer's butterscotch leather couch, which is now draped with a leopard throw to conceal the dried bloodstain I created when I didn't realize I was bleeding days after the miscarriage—to Spencer's disgust and dismay. He didn't speak to me for a few days after that. Savory scents float in from the kitchen, where Spencer is toiling, cooking me yet another gourmet meal.

"I'd like you to eat from these petite dishes," he says from the kitchen.

I frown.

"I'd rather not," I say. "I'm starving."

Pots clang. I wince. Spencer slams a dish down on the counter so hard it sounds like something cracked.

Then he comes in bearing the food on a tray.

The exotic aromas, the sights, make me deliciously weak—wine-infused gravies and saffron-flavored beans. But what's on the tray, to my amazement, are two miniature dishes no larger than finger bowls.

"Spencer!" I say, my stomach growling at the sight, instantly furious. "I said—"

"Jesus, Rachel, why can't you relax? Why are you so rigid? Come on! Play along, why don't you!"

So this was to be one of his odd rules, or strange games.

"But Spencer . . . this is bullshit. I'm hungry. You made great food. Why can't I just eat it? This is bogus."

He says nothing, sits sternly next to me. Clicks on the TV. I am sullen. Take two bites. That's all that fits in the little dish. Then the fight begins: "You're no fun." "You're a controlling bastard." "You're negative." "You're passive-aggressive." We hurl bilious digs, back and forth, like we're tossing scat. Until it escalates to the point that dishes in the kitchen are left untouched and I storm out of the bungalow, slamming the flimsy door behind me. Stomp to where my truck is parked on Venice Boulevard. Slide in the cab. And fume.

And every time this repeats, I see again my father's back, as he walks out the door of the apartment at West 110th Street. I hear the door slam again, the heavy New York apartment door with its triple locks. My father's back, in a gray-colored trench, his black hair, leaving. Every time I storm off to sit in my truck. I reexperience my father leaving me.

Until I fall asleep. Wake, and walk back to the bungalow and up the ladder and into Spencer's bed, to stroke and soothe, apologize and weep.

This is bliss. Pure fusion and forgiveness—*after* a nasty fight.

Looking back, I see how I was playing my father's role. I would leave. This time, I would be the one retreating. Watch my back as I go.

A memory: I am three, or four. My parents are fighting in the bedroom. Their voices rise, seem to slice into each other. I am in the hallway, playing with dolls. I have a cowboy doll with a removable brown plastic cowboy hat, rubber spurs, and chaps, and I have a pretty, pointy-toed Barbie with rock-hard breasts. As my parents fight, I turn the dolls toward each other. Barbie starts: "You're a bitch," she says. Cowboy moves in closer. "Shut up. Shut your goddamn mouth." Barbie swings her stiff arm up as if she's going to hit Cowboy, who throws down his hat. "I can't take this. I'm leaving," says Cowboy. "Don't you dare," says Barbie, and unlike my mother, who always cries and screams, Barbie stays firm. They are locked in this battle, neither one leaving. I am concentrating so hard on the dolls fighting, on helping them get the words out, inventing a constant steady stream, that what happens is I forget my parents are fighting. After a while, I don't even hear them anymore. I am creating my own drama. I learn later this is literally called "acting out." And there in that hallway, sitting on the hardwood floor amid the dust bunnies and the overflowing bookshelves, the two dolls facing off, I smile. Because this time, I am controlling the chaos. All by myself.

At least, this is how I remember it. Though to hear parents raging at each other could only have filled a child that age with fear. So quickly, then, the survival instincts kick in, the fear morphs into action. Feelings mutate into playacting—a playacting that in adult life will cause serious damage.

A few weeks later, at a dinner party—actually a rotating private supper club called Gents, where the men cook for the women and then the women vote on which is the best dish—Spencer calls out to me from the kitchen.

"Hey, Tits!"

I don't know he is speaking to me. When I realize he is, I am so embarrassed I don't blush—I turn the deep color of terra-cotta.

I say, "Please don't call me that."

"Come on, Tits. Don't be uptight. Where's your sense of humor?"

The other women pause, then keep talking. They do not look at me. All these women are married, and mothers, or about to be mothers. I want to die.

The theme tonight is Japanese. I am wearing pink and black striped thigh-high stockings from Italy, a short swingy skirt, a white button-down shirt with a stretchy pink and black tube top layered over it, a mustard and blue tie, a Japanese beige knitted cap with an angora ball and my hair in pigtails—an aging Japanese schoolgirl kind of getup my friend helped me create.

Spencer is furious when his "boat" filled with shrimp and caviar doesn't win the prize. He's spent days planning and preparing it, and spent money he doesn't have. Appearances are important to him.

I don't remember how his dish tasted. I do remember how spectacular the presentation was, every detail: the red sails made out of flowers, pierced by the wooden mast; the jumbo shrimp flanging the sides of the scooped-out pineapple hull, like tiger-striped prawn paddles, the pretty orange caviar translucent on top of the culinary cargo.

I do remember how the boat looked too heavy to float—on the sea or in the stomach.

What I also remember is this night, after being called "Tits," I got so drunk I walked out of the house before dessert, vomited into the rosebushes, climbed into my truck, and drove to a friend's house. I did not even say good-bye. Not to the hosts. And not to my boyfriend. I hardly remember the drive. It was a Saturday night, the street was thick with traffic, people cruising. I do remember opening the door at a stoplight and puking onto Hollywood Boulevard. I arrived, somehow, barely, at my friend's house. She was not home. Or maybe it was so late she was asleep. I planted myself on the stoop. And I fell asleep there. I woke before dawn, drove back home to a slew of e-mails cursing my very marrow. Calling me a piece of shit, and far worse. And saying it was over.

What did I do? Think of why I might've drunk so much? Consider whether I was even slightly happy? Consider whether I was maybe miserable, taking a slow boat to suicide?

Think again.

I drove right over to Spencer's. And opened the door to the bungalow with my key.

I couldn't let go, because it was all I had. I, Rachel, had disappeared. I had poured every ounce of myself into this vision I had of the perfectly loveable Rachel, the perfect couple, the perfect solution to my so-far botched life. I'd invested everything I had in this fantasy.

I had no choice.

So I climbed up the ladder, crawled into bed with this man. And I wept and said I was so sorry, so sorry, so sorry, I am a piece of shit, I am a fuck-up, I don't know what happened to me, I love you so much, I don't deserve you, let me prove myself, give me another chance. And I massaged his back and his neck and his arms and his whole steel-coiled, steroidally pumped and ripped body, even though he lay there like a slab of Kobe beef and said not a word, not until many hours had passed, many, many hours—and my fingers and back and neck were sore, aching, and I wanted to vomit up my entire being, every last shred of dignity. He didn't even let out a sound when I gave him a blow job, tonguing the skin of his uncircumcised cock with devotional fervor until he came so hard his whole body quaked. By the time he spoke, and said, "I'll consider continuing to see you," I was a sodden wreck.

Only then did I breathe again.

And this happened more than once.

One day I am having coffee with my friend Dylan, a reserved and elegant writer who is slender as a butter knife. She is wearing a pair of jeans the saleslady at the consignment shop said used to be owned by Paris Hilton. They are gloriously ripped and bejeweled and studded.

"I had to take them in!" she says with delight.

"Dylan, you can't live on air. Did you remember to eat today?" I smile, but Dylan is so sharp, she catches on right away.

"How are things with Spencer?" she says carefully.

I sigh. Then I launch into a watered-down version of our latest fight.

Dylan doesn't say it—she's too restrained and delicate, too conscious of overstepping—but I can see she registers the hurt and sadness I know is obvious in my face. I have learned so much from her in the few years we've been friends.

"Rachel, do you find yourself apologizing all the time?"

"Yes," I say. Relieved to be asked the right question. I wasn't ready to explore what the question pointed toward—not yet. But I would remember it when I was.

Spencer breaks up with me. This time for good.

"You know, this shouldn't have lasted more than a couple months."

"Do you mean we can't even sleep together? But I need you. I love you!"

Spencer says, "If it weren't for your forcing this with your strong personality, it would've been over a long time ago."

I try to salvage the relationship. Again. But this time, he does not answer my calls. He does not answer my e-mails. And yet, he is all I can think about. I'm jonesing. My drug routes are blocked, my escape routes are sealed. I'm officially smacked down; I have finally hit my personal bottom.

I can't take it anymore. I'm worn out. I'm scarred. I've spilled all the blood I can spill.

I am empty. Hollow. A clattering shell. A bone with all the marrow scooped out.

I surrender.

A friend mentions there are twelve-step meetings for people who have problems with love, sex, fantasy, and romance. For decades, I've gone to support-group meetings of people affected by alcoholism. But somehow, I kept making the same mistakes over and over with my relationships.

Until Spencer.

I do the only thing I can think to do.

I go to a meeting.

A meeting for people who can't figure out sex, or love, or romance to save their lives.

CHAPTER EIGHT
Recovery

2005

The guy next to me coughs. I hold my bag in my lap, cross my arms, press my bare legs together. What was I thinking, wearing a skirt? Like this is some kind of sick tea party. There are about thirty of us gathered in a small room at a community center. Lawn bowling trophies line dusty glassed-in shelves. Every person here looks like a freak—seedy, uneasy, sad, afflicted with either roving eye or the inability to even look up from the scuffed floor. At least, that's how I see things in my fragile, psychically naked state. Hair on my neck prickles. Another guy scrapes his chair and I jump. If I could leave my skin, if I could pluck out my eyes, if I could wrap myself in an invisible-making cloak or even hide myself inside a portable phone booth—anything but be here, exposed—I would.

I am at my first support group meeting for people who have trouble with sex and love, fantasy and romance. Who have so much trouble they call themselves addicts because they fix on this stuff like others do with drugs, or food, or drink. Why am I here? If you've read this far, I think you know.

Because I don't know what else to do. Because I'm desperate. Because if I meet another Spencer, I can see myself going down the road my mother took.

One woman seated against the far wall wears a plunging pink rayon V-neck, tight jeans. But it is her feet I notice most of all. Her shoes. The presentation. Not only are her teetery leopard-print mules worn down at the heel, and the fabric fraying, but her feet are callused, the heels dirty. Even the toenails sport chipped red polish. Somehow this makes me incredibly sad. The way her stomach flows so hopefully, earnestly, over her waistband. The obvious effort, however slipshod the result. The nakedness of her need.

I recognize myself, even if I do drop hundreds on designer shoes and swear by pedicures. The vibe is the same. She feels me looking, glances my way, shooting mild mascara-ed rays of hostility. The kind you shoot at women who're on your turf, who might steal your man. This I recognize, but do not share. I have always loved women. Avoided competing, or at least tried to avoid. I may have always wanted attention. Craved it. But I believe I would not throw over another woman for that hit.

I feel all male eyes on me—at least I believe I do. And to be honest, I like it. There's the familiar buzz, however muted. And when I sink into this feeling, I find I can remain seated.

It is only in looking back that I see the irony. You don't send an alcoholic to a fully stocked bar to meet with other alkies, or overeater groups to a candy shop. But here we are, we love junkies, gathered together, in close quarters, with other people who yearn to flirt and fall in love with and/or fuck us, as much as we want to do the same. Wobbly as I was, I remember that jungly primal tension being too thick to cut even with a machete for many, many months. That first day, I had no idea what was up.

Everyone introduces themselves. Identifies themselves. Whatever their weakness or addiction. One after another says, "Hi, I'm So-and-so, and I'm a romance addict," or, "Hi, I'm Blankety-blank, and I'm a sex addict."

Then it's my turn.

Blushing, paling, my voice unusually soft, I say, "I'm Rachel. I don't know what I am."

But in my journal that night, I record the truth:

"Oh. My. God. I am a fucking addict."

"I got in my head, my boyfriend and I were going to be Anaïs Nin and Henry Miller all over again," the woman says. Her breathy voice is wry, confident, smart. I sit upright in my chair. She is leading the Saturday-morning meeting, and she is speaking right to me. Even the way her hair spills from her scalp in hopeful hennaed locks, the way her shirt is misbuttoned and gaps open at her ample waist, breaks my heart.

"Would you be my first sponsor?" I say to her afterward. I'll call her Vicky.

Vicky and I set bottom lines for things that would be dangerous for me if I want to break this love addiction:

1. No contact with Spencer, other than legal
2. No sex (outside of a committed relationship)

3. No intriguing (manipulating to arouse the interest and attraction of men)
4. No contact with men who trigger
5. Minimum one meeting per week; maximum three meetings per week
6. No conversations with men over one minute

I fold the paper with my bottom lines into my wallet.

Withdrawing from love and sex can be every bit as dangerous as from drugs, where the slightest thing can set the mechanism of addiction right back in motion. For a heroin addict, it could be a spoonful of cough syrup. For a love junkie, it could be one seemingly harmless flirtation. And wham, you're at square one again, in the deadly cycle of obsession, fruitless yearning, and denial.

The antidotes are simple according to this program: Set your personal bottom lines, enlist the help of a sponsor, go to a ton of meetings, make outreach calls, and above all, work the steps. The twelve steps are stages of personal, spiritual, and psychological growth, each with its own focus and flavor. Early steps are about admitting that we can't control the universe, let alone the object of our love, and accepting that we are broken. They are also about illuminating the fact that our best thinking has only brought us pain and that surrendering to something bigger than us will help us change. Other steps require us to dig deep, excavate our past behaviors, recognize our patterns of addiction, take our own moral inventory. The program suggests we share what we learn about ourselves in these inventories with someone else in the program. It is a kind of purging.

Later steps encourage us to stay on this path by seeking spiritual guidance, taking responsibility for our actions and our lives, being of service. And ultimately, returning to a sense of community, interconnectedness, healthy intimacy, and wholeness.

At least, that's the rough idea. Easier said than done.

From that point on, I go to meetings two or three times a week. I don't know what's happening, exactly, but I am now able to recognize that buzzy force field around certain people. And to avoid getting involved with them. I am finding I actually enjoy being alone.

One day, in a meeting, I hear this: "Addiction is avoiding creative responsibility."

This line will haunt and guide me as I step gingerly onto a new path. One that I will fight along the way. Giving up old habits challenges my very sense of self.

"You haven't been checking in with me," says Vicky.

The Saturday meeting has just ended. I was trying to duck out before Vicky saw me. "I don't know if I can do this," I say darkly. "I feel like I'm wasting my libido. Wasting time. A chance to connect with someone. Like this is some kind of cult against hedonism. Anti-love. You know?"

"I know," she says. Then she tells me how she is seeing a man who is drinking heavily and using drugs. I nod, understanding. "He lives in his car," she says. "And he's married. But we have something special." She takes my hand. "So I understand."

I look at Vicky, and for a second, I see Jane. The way I used to see my mother's face in stray dogs, or homeless people when I first came to Los Angeles. I'm not talking about resemblance—I mean seeing my mother's face in the flesh, human or dog.

I don't call Vicky again. I don't tell her clearly, and maturely, that I think it best if I move on to another sponsor, but thank you for the help you've given so generously—and I am not proud of that avoidance. Without a sponsor, someone supposedly with more experience in these meetings and recovery, someone who can help steer me, I let my guard down during socializing post-meetings.

After one Saturday meeting, a group of us love junkies gather at Snug Harbor, a cozy breakfast joint nearby. I'm sucking down my third cup of joe, and chowing on some heavily syruped French toast. There have to be some pleasures in life. There's a cute guy sitting right across from me; I know I'm not supposed to look at him, for too long, but I am hyperaware when he's looking at me and I know we have some kind of energy. I figure this is okay, because we're all honest about our addiction. We know about respect. And boundaries. We're conscious, right? Maybe he and I, we're meant to be an item down the line. After some more recovery, whatever that is. The men sit near each other, while the women clump together on the opposite side of the table. I feel like I'm in junior high.

Us girls giggle. Gossip about what someone's shared at the meeting. Jennifer, a doe-eyed ex-beauty who's now a little rough around the edges, leans in to whisper sharply, "You think you're all recovered because you've come to a few months of meetings? You think that's how it works? This program is deep. You're not even at step one. I see you flirting across the table. That's totally fucked-up."

I turn and look at her in surprise. My appetite is shot. I shut my mouth, fold into myself, and the weird gripping darkness I've been feeling since I started these meetings spreads throughout my body. I hate all of this. I understand nothing.

"Meetings are like parties," one woman tells me when I call her from the phone list. She has been coming for seven years, an eternity in these groups. "Depending on the host, and the guests, the tone can change. Maybe try to find one that feels more comfortable."

She also says to me, "Maybe that meeting was bringing out your addict. The worst in you. All your judgment and harshness. Is the way you saw everyone there possibly how you see yourself?"

I start going to a small afternoon meeting in the Valley. Everyone is quiet. Meditative. Serious about getting better. And mostly married or in relationships. And older. This does not feel like junior high. This does not feel like a coalition of mean girls, desperate for male attention, with me the meanest and most desperate of all. Now I start hearing what people are saying. And the rawness, the honesty, is like a baptism. A natural purification. Everyone shares about how they are damaged. Everyone listens. And I swear, I can even feel the healing . . . however slow and invisible.

For many months, I hole up in my Topanga hideaway, and I cry. I'm embarrassed to say this. I've always considered myself a tough girl, but the truth is, I've never cried so much. Curled up, with all the windows closed so no one can hear me, the quilt cocooning my body, which doesn't even feel like my body anymore, it's so quiet and untouched by others' hands, I let out gut-wrenching sobs. The kind that rack your body and squeeze your stomach tight. For months, these jags don't make me feel better. I feel emptied. Lost.

Then one day, a thought rises up in the midst of all that sobbing:

No one is going to save you.

And that is when the emptiness of my body, and the bankruptcy of my yearnings, starts to feel like a kind of lightness. A liberation. No one is going to save me, and for the first time, I am getting an inkling that maybe I don't need anyone to do that job.

My brother is coming to Los Angeles to visit me.

I have not seen him in ten years.

In the six months since I have pulled back from all the men, the crushes, the relationships, the pursuits, the obsession with finding true love, finding the father of my child that I am positive I'm meant to have, I have created more space for other things, other people, more centered relationships.

Like family.

My brother finds me blading on Venice Beach. I'm suited up in shiny silver sweatpants, gold jewelry, and a tight tank top. Does he think I look like a clown? A fashion diva? A ditz?

My brother, however, is sweating more than I am, stuffed

into ill-fitting cargo pants and a T-shirt he keeps self-consciously plucking away from his chest.

I am wearing gold eye shadow and a lunatic lip-glossed smile to hide my discomfort.

I wonder if he flinches when he looks at me.

Does he see a loudmouthed and vain middle-aged woman trying too hard? How about the cherry red metallic pickup truck? Does it remind him of the green truck our mother drove? Often into trees? What about, when we get home, my homicidal scarlet macaw?

All this flashes through my brain in an instant as I study the baby brother I haven't seen in a decade.

Michael drives an economy rental car that is too small for his six-foot-four frame, with many new pounds, his brown hair long, unwashed, and stringing loose around the intense face. I'm ashamed to report I recoil.

Then it hits me with a psychic uppercut: He had it worse growing up. Far worse. It's what I always say to him, but I didn't expect it to be so physically manifest.

When things fell apart, he was only a baby. Angelic. Eight years my junior, with his String up his nose.

I realize I hardly know my brother, and he hardly knows me.

We embrace awkwardly and I zip my mouth. I swallow my disappointment in his appearance. I'm afraid it is a sign that he is emotionally crippled, but I hold on to possibility.

"Tell me things about you," I say. We're sitting on my deck overlooking Topanga State Park.

"In my youth, I used mushrooms in a sacramental fashion, to

unlock all the locks and chains and cogs and wheels." This is how my brother talks.

"Remember that time," he says, "when Cousin Lou hit me in the knee with a plastic rake?"

"I remember! Jane sat you in her lap and poured her beer into the wound."

"And said, 'There! That'll fix it!'"

We laugh so hard the deck shakes.

Then he turns to me and speaks urgently.

"Our mother left me alone a lot, Rachel, after you went away. One time, it was one day, then two days. I didn't know where she was. I was a baby, and I was starving for food. She left me by myself in the barn where we used to live. I figured out how to open the window, climbed out, crawled down the stairs, crawled down the dirt road to the main house to scrounge for food."

I want to save my brother, but it is too late. All I can do now is love him. When I look over and see Michael sitting on my deck, it is the most beautiful thing I've ever seen. I feel a dizzying rush of humanity, and then I see an unvarnished truth: For years I have been so obsessed, so preoccupied with my need for a fix, I have ignored my own brother.

If love is like heroin, then swearing off all the behavior associated with love, for a time, as an experiment, might constitute withdrawal. Withdrawal from a process, not a drug. But a withdrawal, with chemical consequences, and psychological ones, just the same.

One of the things I learn in these meetings is how not to

indulge in these love highs, whatever form they take. No dates. No casual sex. No fantasizing, even. Mine are varied. I try to cut back almost everything.

I return to the Saturday-morning meeting. This time, I don't see sleaze. I don't even see desperation. I see a group of people, reaching out. And it is glorious.

One way I get through withdrawal is to reclaim my creativity. I write a short novel.

The inspiration for it is an old, out-of-print romantic pulp written by a lesbian adopting a male protagonist's point of view. For a change, I write as a man. And not just any male. A conflicted male, with a fabulous, smart fiancée—and a cheesy, sexy, troubled airhead mistress. And a close friend with whom there are unspoken homosexual undertones.

For four months, I channel every which way of indulging love junkie impulses through this character. I even invent hedonistic pleasure palaces in nearby Santa Monica. Maybe what I'm writing is nothing more than an updated version of the homemade porn I drew as a kid. But it is tangible proof I am not avoiding creative responsibility anymore; I think it also helped me avoid doing the same things in real life.

Because before I knew it, I had two and a half years of almost pure abstinence.

Except for three slips.

Slip Number One: James, a former preacher turned environmental protection agent and charismatic stand-up poet from Georgia, already a grandfather.

Slip Number Two: Miles, a lusty, talented abstract painter from Philly with a noisome yen for young models.

Slip Number Three: Scott, a soft-spoken, earnest, talented musician from Hermosa Beach who wanted to keep the encounter in the "other dimension."

The difference is, they are all friends. We talk honestly. I don't write them thirty e-mails a day, or stalk them by phone. And the slips don't segue into imagined relationships or years-long obsessions.

I just might be making a little bit of progress.

I start a new business, combining my love of travel with teaching writing. A friend happens to have a castle in France, where I organize a writing retreat. Before I leave, I make a painful decision.

Appalled at my scars, and the attacks that keep yielding more serious wounds, I also realize it's time to place Ajax, the homicidal scarlet macaw, in a sanctuary. Finally. I scramble to find the perfect environment, enlisting the help of Parrots First. I try Buddhist aviaries; they all have waitlists. Then I hear of a new sanctuary nearby and plead for Ajax's inclusion.

Two volunteers come to take Ajax's sleek steel "animal environment" apart. I take him outside in a portable carrier. He slams against it, eyes spinning, ruffling his feathers. I gather all his belongings into shopping bags: his zebra-print blanket, his wooden toys, a couple of water bottles he likes to slam around for the noise, and various treats. I cannot stop weeping; tears stream down my face.

Even though this animal attacked me almost the whole five years I took care of him, I am heartbroken.

Turns out, Ajax doesn't want to be with other birds.

Turns out, he gets placed with a celebrity, who loves him so much he's already in her will. She has an aviary, but instead, he follows her around. Does he attack her? Bite her savagely? "They worked through that," the woman from Parrots First who helped place him says mysteriously when I follow up. I let it drop.

Another family member I reconnect with is my father. This will take longer though. It will be more than two years before I feel I have enough strength to contact him. Getting to this point was much harder than reuniting with my brother. It has required intense step work, diligence with meetings, and soul searching.

It occurs to me that it is time to contact my father the day after I get over a silly crush on someone in the program. When I let go of my brief fixation on this man, somehow an old resentment toward my father also lifts.

I write an e-mail. It is short, sweet, neutral. I apologize for the lapse in communication. Then I mention having needed some time to heal, to work on my own issues and behavior. I say that I hope we can reconnect now in a way that's healthier for both of us. I wish him well, say that I've worried about him. I hope to hear from him, and send him love.

What do I want to happen? I want him to forgive me, to respond from a healthier, saner place. For us to connect in a more pleasant way, now that I've removed my sense of entitlement and belief that he owes me money to help support me and make my life easier after all the childhood hardships, expectations of him being a father, desire to make him suffer for past or current mistakes as I see them.

I want him to invite me into his life. I want him to include me at his children's weddings and births. I want him to visit me in Topanga, where I've lived for more than ten years. I want him to apologize for some things that happened in the past. I want him to love me.

I hit Send on the e-mail to my father, and I hold my breath.

After two weeks without an answer, and wondering whether he even got my e-mail, I call my father on his cell phone.

"Hi, Dad." There is a long pause. I hear the obnoxious blat of car horns, the percussive rat-tat sound of a hundred footfalls, voices. I picture my father walking through lower Manhattan with his long-legged stride, maneuvering deftly through crowds, past dogs. Except his hair is now more silvery, his limbs perhaps less swift. He is sixty-five. Retirement age.

"What do you want?" He says he didn't get an e-mail. He has a new e-mail address, which I take down.

"I'm sorry to be out of touch for so long, Dad. How are you? Are you healthy? Everything okay?"

"Yes. Everything's fine. I'm healthy. Why?" He is curt, his voice cold.

"Dad, let me try to explain. I know this call must seem out of the blue. It wasn't about you. Okay? I needed time. To deal with some of my own personal problems. To get some distance, make some changes in myself, in our dynamic. I got a book deal. I started a business."

The conversation is strained, but we have it. And now the lines are open again.

I feel no resentment, nor entitlement, during our conversation. When for four decades, give or take, I have not only harbored but also nursed those feelings.

I'm beginning to feel something that might suggest transformation.

After two-plus years of silence, my father and I begin an e-mail correspondence.

He catches me up on his life, his family. He has more grandchildren! Four in Israel, three others and a fourth on the way in New York. Only one of his four children with Batsheva is childless.

I ask about his relationship with his father, who is ninety-eight, healthy and hale. "I am banned from my childhood home," he writes back. "I have no contact with my father nor do I care to (though I miss having access to my books!)." He goes on to say, "Rumor has it that I have been disinherited."

Both of my parents, disinherited. Emotionally as much as financially, I think.

When he wishes me a happy New Year, for Rosh Hashanah, I write back to wish him the same, and also Yom Kippur. Are you praying? Atoning? I ask. My father is still a man of prickly contradictions, a man who teaches Talmud yet tells me in an e-mail, around Yom Kippur, "I am not big on repentance and asking God for forgiveness—if anything, I think the divinity should be asking forgiveness from human beings for the mess that is religion."

Yet one thing I am so grateful for is that he acknowledges my mother's birthday. Her death. And Mother's Day. He is the only one in our family who seems to remember her, and contacts me about that shared memory. Other than my aunt Annie, Jane's little sister, and my brother, Michael, whom I always have to call.

When I was younger, I saw an ad campaign in the Manhattan subway. I don't remember what it was for. Stop Crime? Stop the Violence? There was a photograph of a man in the ad, a close-up of his face, and on that face a pair of shattered glasses.

I would study that picture and worry about my father. My father, with his horn-rimmed librarian glasses, riding the subway alone, sometimes carrying ancient Talmudic texts, sometimes carrying paper bags of money, since he thought it more clever and safer than carrying a wallet. My father, who would bow his head at the kitchen table when his second wife would yell at him. My father, with his love for chocolate, and pastrami, and other sweet and illicit things.

The memory of that ad campaign touches me again now, years later, when I discover the deep love I carry for my father, despite the past. And despite current disappointment.

Because I called my father with a heart full of expectations, and he met only one.

He didn't tell me he was sorry he left me without a dad at age four, though I understand now. He didn't say, I'm sorry I never stood up to Batsheva and insist that you live with us. He didn't say, I'm sorry I placed that want ad when you were a kid. He didn't say, I'm going to visit you in Topanga after ten-plus years of not visiting.

But he did come back to me in the one way he knew. By writing me e-mails, and engaging in talk about books, and writing, and acknowledging my mother.

I realize now my father will never meet, fully, those expectations I had when I reconnected with him. This story of reunion will not yield a pure, perfect love.

And that is okay. The childhood shades of black and white might finally be yielding room for gradations of color.

"How's the dating?" asks someone at a meeting.

"I haven't started."

I am still scared. What if I repeat the same patterns again?

Plus, I am fine holed up in my Topanga Canyon hideaway. Communing with the lizards, finches, ground squirrels, and moths. Gazing serenely at the verdant green of the state park. I am more used to the quiet now. Perhaps I even crave it. I'm not sure that's healthy.

So I work out some guidelines with my new sponsor. And I write up the following rules on a piece of paper. Fold it in four. Slip the rules in the back of my gold-colored wallet. An amulet protecting me against the evil eye of potential bad boys, of dangerous unavailable men.

Here they are:

Dating Do's and Don'ts

Don't spend more than thirty minutes on any one phone call with any man (*especially* considering your time issues.)

Don't spend more than two to three hours on a date with a

man and never more than one hour on a first date.

Make all first dates for coffee. (I know, lame right? But necessary.)

Don't let them pick you up for the first few dates. *Always* meet them somewhere. This is an important one. Don't be alone with them for the first few dates and don't be alone in your house or theirs for at least the first three or four dates.

Keep the sexual energy *out* of the first four or five dates if at all possible. This too is very, very important.

No alcohol.

For the first couple of dates, have somewhere to be so you can keep boundaries with time; maybe ditto with phone.

It doesn't say anything about women.

For four months or so Catherine Reynolds and I are casual friends.

She lives five minutes away from me in the canyon. We meet in a support group for love junkies.

A women's stag meeting.

A meeting I did not want to go to. But my new sponsor suggested it might help with my growth, so I try it.

Catherine always brings the energy up in these meetings with her quick wit and luminous white smile. A native of Mississippi, she has a natural warmth and ease in social gatherings, and even when she talks of painful things, there is something uplifting. And fun. That's it. She seems to have the secret to enjoying life.

Catherine was a Chi Omega sorority girl at Ole Miss. At five foot eleven, I imagine she must've been a scary vision in sweater sets and pearls. I'm sure we wouldn't have spoken, even though she did play college volleyball. Since, she's transformed into a gamine. She avoids makeup, wears vintage concert T-shirts and low-cut designer jeans, cuts her dirty blonde hair in seventies girl rocker style, and lounges in the meetings with a youthful insouciance.

Sometimes we walk down the hill to get coffee at Café Mimosa. Or meet at the Santa Monica stairs to work out. We talk on the phone sometimes. We laugh. We have dinner one night at Chaya.

It's my close friend Anastasia's birthday.

I don't see her so much anymore. Except on our birthdays. Because she married well and is generous, she often treats me to a massage and meal on her birthday.

This time, we are at the exclusive Peninsula Hotel.

"I got you the Masseuse's Choice," Stasia says. "Okay? So it'll be a surprise. I know you're really stressed right now. Surprises are always good."

She knows me so well, sometimes she knows what I need before I do.

When the masseuse walks in, I am struck by her resemblance to Frida Kahlo, only less intense. I remember her having a long thick glossy black braid wound around her head, and warm brown eyes. When she takes my foot in her hand and traces an eight there, she has me.

"What does eight mean to you? I can talk if you want, during the massage. Does eight mean something?"

At first, I'm seeing the eights I used to trace on tabletops when I was a kid. When adults were acting crazy. When I wanted to disappear. Into infinity.

Now it means something different.

I open my mouth, and I don't know what it is, but words tumble out. This woman inspires me to speak. To reveal. Or maybe it's the work I've been doing in recovery. Whatever is going on, I'm vulnerable. Naked under that sheet. Naked-hearted.

"I'm forty-four. Eight is four plus four. So that's what it makes me think of." I pause. She listens, keeps kneading my foot.

"And . . . I want to have a child." She presses her knuckles deep into the sole, rocks them there. Silent.

"And I have so little time left." A tear forms in my eye and drops through the white hole where I'm resting my face.

"I just went to the fertility doctor last week. He will put me on fertility drugs, test my levels, do four or five inseminations, and he says that should work. They stop doing that at age forty-five." I open my eyes, study the neatly swept tile floor beneath the face cradle. "Thing is, I can't afford the treatments today. And I'm afraid I won't have one—that I will never have my own child."

With the heel of her palm, she burrows into a complicated knot between my shoulder blades. I breathe into the pain.

"Maybe," she says, "you will express your maternal instinct in another way from what you thought."

I weep. I weep great racking sobs. Mucus drips through the soft cloth face cradle. Drenches the sheet. Something gets released. Some kind of psychic hairball. I simply can't stop sobbing.

And it is like I am shipwrecked on that crisp white massage table, shipwrecked and saved at the same time.

When I go out to meet Stasia for our gourmet spa lunch on the terrazzo, she is stunned by my appearance.

"Rach, you look like hell. What happened in there?"

"I couldn't stop crying."

"Why?"

"That massage—I don't know. It was life-changing, Stasia. Let's eat first. I'll tell you everything."

The next day, Catherine and I have dinner plans.

"I'll come get you."

Catherine picks me up in her retro Land Cruiser. When I slip into the leather seat, I instantly feel the energy.

Something's shifted.

When she turns toward me, I see she is wearing a dark-colored button-down shirt open deep at her chest. I believe she's even wearing makeup, her tilted brown eyes more dramatic and lively than usual, her skin tanned and lovely, her smile bright as ever. After choosing and tossing a slew of clothes, I'm wearing a brown linen skirt from Italy, swingy on my hips and legs, brown espadrilles, a soft pistachio green T-shirt that bares no cleavage. Possibly a bit dressy for a casual dinner with a casual friend. Modest . . .

And yet . . .

Both of us are awkward.

"Where should we go?"

Buzzy.

"I don't know."

"Wherever you like."

Bit of a rush happening.

"How 'bout Chaya again."

Or am I imagining things?

"Whatever. I don't care."

As we wind through the twilit canyon where we both live, down to the Pacific Coast Highway, where the ocean lies glittering, light dancing off its mild waves, Catherine says suddenly, "Let's go to Malibu." And turns right.

Damn if this doesn't feel like a date.

At Allegria, a cozy Italian joint with a distinctly romantic vibe, Catherine chooses a spot way in the back, a table with low lighting.

I note tonight marks the summer solstice.

As we talk, she stretches her arms upward, revealing a glimpse of a six-pack. This girl has a six-pack. Jesus.

"When did your mother die?" she asks.

"I was fourteen."

"That's where you get all that male energy," she says. "No mother to model on. Those teen years are crucial."

How many girls have washboards? I find myself thinking how hot that is. But the thought is somehow—floating out there. Not yet connected to me. I concentrate on the *penne arrabiata*. Chew.

I realize I am thirteen years older than she is. Roughly the same age difference as Eddie was to me. Does that mean I'm supposed to be the wise one? The authority? The one who sets the tone and keeps it safe? I realize I don't really know how to behave anymore.

"Have you ever been with a woman?" she asks.

My stomach drops down to the basement. Is she hitting on me? No. It's just love junkie curiosity. I also find myself idly wondering if she thinks I'm attractive.

We talk about selfish fathers, clinging mothers.

"Do you think you're attracted to women because you're seeking your mother?" I ask Catherine. Looking back, I realize I was poking around to see if she had a pattern of falling for older women, mother figures—and wondering if I was going to be just another one of those. A mere projection screen in a long line. What I wasn't aware of was how judgmental I was being— or how interested I already was in this woman. This person.

She makes a face. "Not necessarily."

"I think I look for men who're like my father," I say, "and then . . . I play the role of my mother, weeping for the men."

I look at Catherine, sipping her sparkling water.

Neither one of us seems to want to go, even though the other customers leave. Until it is only us still there. And the waiters, clattering dishes, scraping chairs: waiter Morse code for Please Go Home.

"You okay?" she asks.

"Yes, thank you for asking."

What I want to say is, You're sweet. You actually listen. What a shocker.

What I want to say is, Where did you come from?

And yet—I don't trust myself.

I don't trust this.

Not yet.

Finally we leave. We don't say anything. But now the energy is a sheet between us, lustrous and vibrant. A radiant curtain.

When I climb into bed that night, I'm breathless. Confused. Smiling. I don't know why. And I don't understand. At all.

A deer nibbles on some pampas grass a hundred feet off the deck to my left. I think of my mother, how she could not get love from her family. But would not stop trying.

It is easier to weep in the sun. The converging of sunlight, butterflies, hummingbirds makes sadness easier to bear.

Here's another admission: I daydream about fields of phalluses. They are tall and firm, thick and robust with their pulsing visible veins, swaying in the gentle breeze, filling the ground. All different shades and tones, shapes and angles. Regal. Triumphant. Cocky.

At night I dream of penetration. Deep invasions that split me asunder and leave me panting for more. Impalings. The ancient ritual, full of a purifying kind of violence and primalism I crave.

Can I give up men?

I do not know.

I tell Stasia about Catherine, and my doubts.

"Relax. You have trust issues. Anyone's going to bring them up. Just be careful, Rach," says Stasia. "You have a tendency to put too much on people. They can't be antidepressants. People can't be everything."

And so, I cautiously enter a new relationship—without even knowing who I am anymore.

Over the next few months, I get initiated into making love with a woman.

With a friend.

And it is utterly different: steamy, ecstatic, superhot.

Yet gentle.

Catherine is a Christian. A Chi Omega. The kind of girl who doesn't masturbate, because she thinks her dead grandmother is watching her, looking down on her with disapproval and distaste if she so much as thinks about it.

She has a certain modesty I'm missing. Also a sense of privacy. Not to mention delicacy.

She's also, to quote Stasia, "smokin' hot."

I remember how she made the first moves. How she kissed me that first time. And I thought, hell, this won't work. Good! Now I don't have to deal with the weirdness of being involved with a woman. Of having to start all over again as a lover. Of letting go of my hetero bag of tricks I've accumulated with all the men.

The next night, thinking I was safe, I figured, hell, let me kiss her the way I know how to kiss. I can loosen up. Let me just see how this goes.

And damn if it wasn't as hot as with any man.

We stand there on the street, above my place, leaning against her car, our bodies in shadow, the tree frogs making their nightly racket, and we kiss. This time, my mouth is ready. My lips licked wet. I go for it. Allow the attraction I feel for her to motivate my mouth. Seek her tongue. And even though it is small and delicate, darting, her hair soft, her skin softer—the way we lock in together is magic. Something you never ever can predict.

We fit. In every way.

I feel her willowy body pressed against me, the strong flat belly, the small, pert, perfectly shaped naked breasts with the puffy nipples I'd noticed beneath her T-shirts and imagined touching and licking. Now pressed against my ample bosom. Her legs spread wide in a boyish kind of stance. The mixed sensations and details, the gender-bending—the boldness of her enthusiasm, the tight muscles, the eagerness of her tongue, counterpointed by the feminine delicacy of her hands, the slender fingers, the silky curtain of hair—is more intoxicating than I could've imagined from our fifth-grade-esque kiss the night before.

Within seconds, I am soaking wet.

And shocked.

And unable to stop.

It is she who pulls away first, not me.

"You sure don't kiss like a straight girl," she whispers, smiling.

When I go to pull her hair away from the nape of her neck, bow her head back the better to kiss her, she says, "Don't. I don't like that. It hurts."

And I falter.

I am used to rough playfulness. Sex that includes physical grappling, where I can express my strength and not subdue or hurt. Where we can get closer, deeper. No holds barred.

But when Catherine says this, I let go of her hair. Stroke it back softly on her head. Tuck one strand behind her ear. Listen. Kiss her more warmly. Turned on by her honesty.

This is not my pattern. Before, I got turned on by deception. The bigger the lie, the better. I lived for the promise of drama and mutual destruction. I enjoyed knocking down boundaries in the name of passion—not respecting them. Now, I don't even recognize myself. And that's a good thing.

When Catherine finally drives off the few minutes down the hill to her home, I stay standing. Struck dumb. Drowning liquidly in night shadows. Lips tingling. Loins insanely warm.

If this isn't biology, and it isn't fixing, then what is it? Is it abnormal? Is it perverse?

I don't know what comes next, how this works with a woman, but I know I can't resist.

July 4 is the first day we spend together from start to finish. There are barbecues and parties. We committed to them all. But from the moment we meet up, all we can do is talk, and touch, and make out. I am wet just on seeing her. We go to a restaurant, but I can barely eat. I haven't been sleeping. I'm anxious. Wired. Easily upset. I don't want to say it. I ask my friends what's wrong with me. I can't wrap my mind around what is plain to see: I am lovesick.

I worry about the attraction for Catherine. After all, with the men I loved, sex was all we had. It was the centrifugal force. Without it, we were nothing.

Whether Catherine and I will hit a wall and everything will fizzle, sparks fading into the fabric of our mutual night sky, I am not sure.

When we finally make it to my house, fall into the bed, Catherine is no longer as shy. No longer holds back.

"I want to put my mouth on you," she says. "Is that okay?" I nod.

I feel like a virgin.

Imagine my shock when Catherine not only puts her lips on me but mouths a kind of music I've never heard or felt before—joined by a perfect symphony of fingers. The combined sensation: seismic.

Now I understand how women fuck. Maybe the field of phalluses will now wilt, harvested and replaced by a row of slender fingers. What did the ad say? Let the fingers do the walking.

I joke, but I'm overwhelmed.

Once again tears course down my face.

"You okay?" she says.

"More than okay." She holds me in her arms.

My heart is beating, I am sloppy slippery wet, when I finally manage to rouse myself and straddle this woman. Finally facing, buck naked, her female form.

Terrified, filled with lust, and a desire to please her, to reach her, to give—even if I have no idea what I am doing; "I have no idea what I'm doing," I say—I slide languorously down her body, dropping kisses along the way, until I reach her carefully cropped and groomed and scented terrain, take a deep breath, sweep my hair back from my face, and dive down in.

To the unknown.

While I am there, I find myself wondering—as I lose myself in mazes of skin and silken folds of flesh, seeking, nibbling, licking, sucking, searching, blindly, listening avidly to any noise she might make, any word of encouragement, feeling any slight shift of her body or movement, trying to sense her body's responses—how on earth the men did it all. Because what I am also letting guide me, as I work and lick and tease, and alternately bury my head, or press it deeper, is how it would feel for me. Imagining, as much as I can, that I am Catherine, that she is me, and somewhere is down there, and what has worked for me, and how had they done it, and could I replicate it, and letting myself become Catherine—until at long last, to my surprise and utter delight, she lets out a cry, shakes, and I crawl back up to hold her in my arms, as she trembles slightly and breathes softly into my neck.

I can't believe how happy I feel. How surprising this is. I'd like to punch her in the arm to let her know, maybe throw her into a headlock, or wrap her hair in my fist and kiss her neck, but instead, I just smile to myself and gently pull her close.

A few weeks later, in my bed, Catherine recounts one of those random moments when she looked at me and felt her heart swell.

"That's when I realized I was in love with you. I guess I just surrendered to it."

She gazes at me directly. My chest constricts: fear. I don't want to be so vulnerable with someone who's right here. Meeting me.

"I was thinking we should see other people," I say. Like this is something that's been choking my throat, an emotional chicken bone.

She looks at me, stricken. Buries her face in her hands for a second.

"What do you mean?" she says through her fingers. "Your voice completely changed. I don't even know who you are right now."

"I just was thinking, I mean—I'm trying to be slow about all this and savor and . . . I don't know, make sure that . . . I'd thought of it before and wanted to . . ." I shut my mouth. She's right. I said the same exact thing to Eddie. Yet unlike Eddie, this woman is open, she seems capable of love. And I have just pushed her away, because I was relating not to her, but to a ghost. This is a bigger slip than sleeping with someone. Clearly I'm the screwed-up one here. The good news is, I catch myself.

"It's okay," she says after a while. "I know you're scared. I am too."

Anastasia wants to know gory graphic details. She wants to know how it all works too. But for once, I'm not in the mood to dish. This relationship feels different. I don't want to expose all the private moments. Before, I had always loved talking about the sex—and maybe that was another form of exhibitionism. What I have with this woman feels sacred. Because there is an actual intimacy. Something I always wanted to have but never felt before.

"She asked me to go steady," I tell Stasia. "And I said yes. It all feels like a return to innocence."

I tell her how the turn-on is not constant.

I don't know if this is because it's a woman, or because it's not addictive.

Or because one minute she's my friend, next she's my lover. Transformed. The aspects fused. Or because we connect in so many ways the sex isn't the only chance at closeness.

What I do know is, our desire ebbs and flows. And that this is beautiful.

Unlike other relationships, I don't feel the lust swamping everything. Or an almost infantile greed and desperation driving that lust.

What I realize is, this feels sustainable.

What I realize is, I have never felt more satisfied.

"How're things with Catherine?" Stasia asks another day.

"What do you mean?"

"I mean, how's it going?"

"Fine." I pause. "Good, I guess. I don't know. I haven't thought about it." I sound perplexed. And I am. On so many levels. I still don't know who I am. Who am I when I'm not shooting up love?

"See! That's how it is with my husband. Sounds healthy. You know, Rach, this is what it used to be with you. Your relationships would be in stages. Stage one: the high. Everything was amazing, incredible, earthshaking. Stage two: conflict and drama. Stage three: SOS. All the calls would be emergencies. And stage four: tearful hellish breakups."

It's true, I never could stand the leaving part.

It is now eight months since things started with Catherine. I am standing outside my home in Topanga, bright red blood streaming from my right wrist, splattering onto the brick walkway by my feet. A crow is cawing behind me. Otherwise, the canyon is so quiet I can hear the drops hitting brick.

It's not what you think.

Moments before, I came home to find my place locked. I'd forgotten my house keys in my rush to visit Catherine. For the past few days, she'd been pulling away. I felt, after eight months of letting her make more of the effort, it was my turn to show up. To let her know I wanted to be in this. That I was willing to work on whatever needed to be worked on. I figured, maybe this was how it worked for normal people. You couldn't avoid fighting altogether, could you? I'd always heard relationships were hard.

Underneath my thoughts: a primal, unconscious fear of abandonment. The great motivator.

"We need to talk," Catherine says when I get to her place. I sit down next to her on the couch. "Your negativity is getting in the way," she begins. I feel my brow knit together, my eyes narrow. Tears gather in Catherine's eyes. "This is hard for me. It's so scary. I don't know how you're going to take this, Rachel." She pauses, wipes her eyes with the back of her hand. "I think you're addicted to misery."

I don't remember what else happens. I jump to my feet. Spit something out like, "Well, fine, if that's how you feel, then I'll just leave." Bang the door behind me. Speed home, blood boiling as I tear around the canyon curves. I see my house is locked and decide I will hit the heel of my hand on the bedroom window—the same window Spencer used to break in to my home—pop the glass so it will slide over on the runners and then I can climb in. I've done it dozens of times before. All you have to do is find the correct spot.

This time the window shatters under my pounding.

Let me pause here. What went wrong? I remember banging on the window, trying to get it to move. Expecting it to pop right away like it always had. And when it didn't—I must've hit that window so hard that it splintered under my blows, burst into cracks and shards, one of which sliced right into my wrist.

Why did it happen? Because I was seething.

I step back. Startled. Look down, and feel instantly queasy. There is a gash in my right wrist so deep I can see what I think is white bone. I stumble backward, dizzy. I don't remember what happens next. Somehow I am upstairs in my landlords' bathroom and they are bandaging the wound, wrapping my wrist.

Then I call Catherine.

She comes right over to drive me to a nearby urgent-care center in Malibu. Romantic Malibu.

This does not feel like a date.

The wound requires five stitches.

"You don't know your own strength," Catherine says. "Do you know you always slam car doors?"

I don't know. What else don't I know? A lot. If I am in recovery from being a full-blown love junkie, I guess I've only gotten as far as the foyer.

CHAPTER NINE
Grief

1977

I'm about to do my special dive, the reverse full gainer. It's midsummer, and I have the walk perfectly mapped out, know where the sweet spot of the board is. I center myself, feeling the nubs of the white diving board under my wrinkly bare feet, snap the racer-back strap of my Speedo. The stretchy material feels good on my shoulders, tanned and a little sore from the sun. The suit somehow holds me tight, holds me together, makes me feel slick and strong as a dolphin. The smell of chlorine is like camphor, or smelling salts. Instantly reviving. Even thrilling. The judges are sitting there in their folding chairs, score cards and pens in their laps. I smile, flex my muscles, shake them out. Now I'm ready to make my approach, step, step, step, looong step, and up, one leg bent and bounce down and vault up into the sky-blue air—go!

Which is when I spot her. Her and him. A woman dressed in rags, with hollowed scary eyes, hair frizzed and flyaway, the jean jacket and jeans, boots, T-shirt, and a small boy, a blond boy, close by her side. She holds him tightly by the hand.

My mother.

And my brother.

I'm in Cranford, New Jersey. My mother lost custody of me months ago. She doesn't live here. She lives in Massachusetts. What's she doing here? And what is my brother doing here? He went to live with his father in Delaware when she lost custody of him. My head is spinning, and I'm losing concentration. This all happens in an instant.

"Let's go!" shout-whispers my coach. "You can do it!"

That's not what my mother says. When she called me last week at the house where I live, at the gym teacher's, and asked how I was, I said, "I'm fine. I won the spelling bee. I have great friends. I'm diving. I'm playing field hockey. I'm doing great in school."

And she said, "That's wonderful, Rachel." And paused. Then, her voice heavy and sad, she said, "But I know you're fucked-up inside."

I turn back to the board, try to focus, but I'm furious. Why is she here? Focus—picture the dive in my head, the tiny splash only large enough for my pointed feet to plunge through—then I go. Goddammit, I go. Nothing can stop me.

And I hit the sweet spot, only I'm a little off, my placement is too far to the right, and I hit wrong and I don't go up so high. And when I reach up and out to the sky, away from the board, and flip back toward the board, I hit that board with my heel. The dull irreversible shock of it, the sound of it, blunt and unmistakable, makes me think I am going to die right there. I panic. It could've been my head; next time it will be my head. I cannot dive. What was I thinking, diving? I'm a fool. Clumsy and stupid, a bad athlete, a bad girl, a bad daughter. A fucked-up piece of shit. A bitch. That's what my mother said when I used to live with her, when she was drunk.

My feet go in, but they are flat and slap the water, and a cascade splashes up all around me and my angle is wrong so even more water swells up and swishes over, staining the concrete poolside, and then I go under.

The silent pool, the chlorinated baptismal water, the underneath. I stay down as long as I can, hold my breath as long as I can so I don't have to return. I stay down so long my lungs feel as big as balloons, and my head is woozy. But finally I burst up through the surface, to the roar of the crowd, the claps, the "oohs" and "aahs" and "Is she all right?"—and the unmistakable call of my mother, low-pitched, loud and dramatic:

"Rachel! Rachel! Your brother wants to see you!"

I walk right past the coach and teammates, not deigning to hobble, not acknowledging the shooting pain in my heel.

"Just a minute," I say. "I'm fine," I say. "No problem," I say, and I walk over to my mother. I avoid looking at my beloved brother, my young protégé, that blond angel who's always picking his nose, because then I won't be able to say what I need to:

"Get out. Go away. I didn't ask you to come. I didn't even know you were in town. Leave me alone. I don't live with you anymore. I don't want to see you. You make me feel awful. You ruin everything."

And I turn on my heel—the good one—but not before I have seen my mother begin to cry, and not fast enough to avoid hearing those tears that tunnel and funnel through my ears and into my esophagus and burrow under my skin and mingle with the chlorine and stain me forever with guilt and shame and grief and stuff I don't even know I'm accumulating then.

Because all I fucking want to do is survive, and get some straight 8s in a diving meet for the one dive I'm most famous for, that reverse full gainer, that not everyone can do, that requires confidence and courage—and I don't want to turn into anything even remotely resembling my mother. And I think maybe if I jump high enough on the diving board, and spin enough times, and execute enough perfect dives, and leave very little splash behind, then maybe, just maybe, people won't notice that my mother is my mother, and I can just be me.

That was the last time I saw her before she died.

This is what my brother remembers about the night my mother died.

There is a knock at the door at our grandparents' house in Dover, Massachusetts. My brother and my mother are there.

My brother remembers two cops at the door. One sits with him in the living room. Michael sits on the couch with the cop, who offers him a glass of milk. "I swear it was drugged, Rachel. I fell asleep in minutes." Before he fell asleep, though, he heard the cop in the kitchen yelling at Jane. And her yelling back, and crying.

When Michael wakes up, he is in the bathroom. Grannie and Grandfather are there.

"Where's my mother?" Michael asks.

Grannie answers, "She's gone away."

My brother says nobody ever told him what happened. He didn't find out until years later. The hurt in his voice pains me.

We have both speculated for years, suspecting foul play on the part of the family. Perhaps preferring that to facing the brutal truth. And truly feeling it.

"Even if they sent those cops just to harass her, you don't do that with a woman who's unstable, on New Year's Eve. You know what might happen," I say, after I've made him tell the story about the two cops one more time.

"Exactly," says my brother. "That's when the highest number of suicides occur. During holidays."

But now, when I think about the fragment of the letter I received not long ago from Aunt Annie, in which Jane talks about "the unscrupulous use of my two children to punish and diminish me, to deprive me of purpose, of hope," I wonder if the cops simply traced Jane down, confronted her about the kidnapping of her own son when she kept him illegally after an Easter visit, and threatened to take Michael away and return him to his legal guardians that fateful night. I wonder if the prospect of losing both her children was too much. If Jane felt her whole identity, her very purpose in life, was at stake. What was she, if not a mother? And if, rather than make any psychological change, she chose physical death.

Which would mean that my mother was responsible. She chose to die.

She chose to leave us.

And that shatters my heart.

*   *   *

238

"Your father's here to pick you up for your dentist appointment," says the teacher on the day that everything turns gray. It is 1978.

We're in a classroom, but I can't remember which one. All I know is it is eighth grade, I'm a spelling bee champ living with the Greens, the cheerful foster family my father found through the want ad he placed in the *Cranford Chronicle*, I've secretly kissed Andrew Cast, and I'm fourteen years old.

One quick frown before I gather my things. Then I smile at the teacher, wave at my friends, and leave, careful not to reveal my dread.

I don't have a dentist appointment.

In front of the school idles my father's black and white Galaxy Electra 225. Exhaust jets out of the muffler, thick as a Jersey factory smokestack, curdling gray in the cold January air. I like this car. The shocks are shot, so when you ride in it, it feels like you're bouncing along on tipsy waves. It's like a weird barge that's about to sink.

The passenger-side door is already open.

My father never does this. He's always worried he's going to get a hernia, so no lifting or jerking. Including heavy car doors.

I slide onto the worn black vinyl seats, books pressed tight against my chest, heart pounding, sweat trickling down my spine. I sit very straight.

"Dad, I don't have a dentist appointment," I say.

"Your mother's dead," he says. He pulls out of the school driveway. The car floats over the road like it's completely lost traction.

Before my father can say another word, before either of us can so much as blink, I see it. I see my mother in the foster family's house where I live.

She is hanging by her neck in the picture window of the Greens' living room on Union Street in Cranford, New Jersey. The rope creaks as she sways heavily against the ugly yellow drapes. Even from here I can tell she hasn't washed her uniform of worn jeans and torn-up Levi's jean jacket in weeks. Cracked brown cowboy boots scrape slowly over the wood floor.

"She died New Year's Eve," says my father. "She hanged herself." He pauses. "I knew this was going to happen."

"Where?" I say, heart jackhammering against my rib cage.

"In her parents' house. In Dover."

He tells me how she did it, with a rope. That her mother found her in the attic of their home, hanging from the rafters.

The attic, where I used to play for hours with pieces of the *Mayflower*. Small bits of wood, bound with string and official cards announcing their authenticity. Where I fingered wafer-thin gold coins, and dug through mysterious old English postcards, exotic stamps. Where I soothed my mother's child-hood stuffed animal Bootsie the goat, her hide gnawed by moths.

I listen. I'm not moving. The car floats. The books are glued to me. My hands are glued to the books. The world is glued, gray, and ungluing.

And it is like someone had stuck a siphon in my head, my heart, every vein and artery, every intestinal coil, and sucked everything out.

There is nothing inside me.

Looking back, I can't explain the vision I had of my mother hanging in the window of the Greens' living room before my father told me how she died. Maybe it seems hard to believe. Later, I learned that shock can do strange things to people's memories. It's possible my father told me that my mother hanged herself, and *then* I saw her dead in the house where I lived. Maybe I thought she chose to die there as a big fuck-you for turning my back on her. It's also possible that I had this vision the way I remember it now—so clearly, so vividly, without any prompting from my father. I will leave it here as a testament to that moment in time. Now I will return to the girl I was, age fourteen, sitting in the Electra 225 with her father. Empty.

"We'll go to the funeral together."

I turn to look at him, but he keeps his profile to me.

"Batsheva said you could?"

My father is coming with me!

Then it hits me, why, what's happening.

And everything turns gray again.

Years later, on a visit to my mother's grave in Dover, the Highland Cemetery caretaker tells me something I don't know.

"Your mother has a secret admirer," he says, winking. We are standing in the shade of an oak tree, in the hush of the well-tended cemetery.

"A secret admirer?"

"He comes on your mother's birthday, every year. And he lays a bouquet of red roses on her grave. And he stays for an hour."

This caretaker is now retired.

And I have never been to my mother's grave on her birthday.

I smell again the fresh-mown grass of Highland Cemetery, see the carefully trimmed spruce trees, the curving drive, the tombstones. I make my way slowly toward the back of the cemetery, toward the stone wall and beyond it the cedar fence and open fields. Then I see the rose quartz marking my mother's grave, a blush of pink visible in the grass. I hope the secret admirer still visits.

GRATITUDE

This book would not exist if it weren't for the fiery and talented Samantha Dunn. When I was in despair, she convinced me to resurrect this project. She guided me in the art of memoir, buoyed me when the material weighed me down, and fueled me with faith that this was a story that needed to be told. I am forever grateful. Then I had the perfect along-the-way reader and editor, Kathleen Fairweather. She read my fresh pages quickly and hungrily each day, asking for more and nudging me when I didn't deliver. In many ways I wrote this for her. The exquisite writer Dylan Landis took the raw draft and cut it with graciousness of spirit and the expertise of a master surgeon. She also provided crucial moral support for the duration of the writing. Elizabeth Hill generously read all along the way too, and offered invaluable insights into this addiction. She always steered me toward honest self-examination, even when I resisted, and inspired me to write a stronger book. She gets a purple heart for putting up with me during the difficult emotional journey this book required. Noelle McCamish was a vital sounding board, and Marilee Albert, my former partner in crime, was a daily source of comfort, encouragement, and pure friendship. I am blessed to have these talented and generous spirits in my life.

Many books and articles informed and influenced my thinking during the often painful process of self-examination, among them *Ready to Heal*, by Kelly McDaniel; *Facing Love Addiction*, by Pia Mellody; *Labyrinth of Desire*, by Rosemary Sullivan; *Why We Love*, by Helen Fisher; *Motherless Daughters*, by Hope Edelman; *Silently Seduced*, by Kenneth M. Adams; *Loss*, by John Bowlby; and *Becoming Attached*, by Robert Karen.

Then there is family. My brother and my father were essential to this book. My brother is a constant source of inspiration and love. My father instilled in me the love of text and the joy of reading. He was unwavering in his support of me seeking the truth at whatever cost.

I want to thank the courageous men and women I've met in the twelve-step rooms who've inspired me with their struggles and stories, and who led me as I embarked on this path of recovery. You know who you are.

I am especially grateful to the different families who were kind enough to open their homes to me when I was growing up. My memories may not be the best, but I believe now that they were all well-intentioned, warm-hearted, and decent people.

Many other essential friends sustained me: Bruce Bauman, Susan Bernard, Francesca Lia Block, Amory Fay, Janet Fitch, Christina Haag, Kristen Herbert, Lou Mathews, Bronnie Milovsky, Anne-Marie O'Connor, Jamie Rose, Chris Solimine, Rob Spillman, Laurie Traktman, Bett Williams, Suzan Woodruff, Margaret Wrinkle.

I also want to thank Linda Renaud, Lisa Firestone, and Sukeshi O'Neal for their steady and generous backing of

Writers on Fire, Linda and Daryl Reynolds for graciously sharing their house in paradise, and Lisa for introducing me to surfing. These tropical creative good times were highlights of this writing year.

Heartfelt thanks also to Jim Fitzgerald; my aunt, Susan Noftsker, and Abbott Fay, for sending me my mother's letters; Diane Hosie-Carolan for keeping me blonde and optimistic; Frankie O'Connell for keeping me well-coiffed; Liz Dubelman; Vicki Whicker; Blair Tindall; Seth Greenland; Hope Edelman; Megan Hollingshead; Frank Sennett; Lima; Ajax; and of course, Juliet.

I want to thank the following movers and shakers: My wonderful agent, Pilar Queen, whose enthusiasm and positivity never faltered. Lindsay Sagnette, for believing in this book when it was still only an idea. Kathy Belden, who shepherded the book with energy and expertise. I feel supremely lucky to have had her as my hands-on editor. Jim Stein for his ongoing faith; Alan J. Kaufman for his legal guidance, creativity, and humor; Alexis Hurley for keeping the torch burning; Maureen Klier for her superb copyediting; all the staff at Bloomsbury USA, with a special thanks to Greg Villepique and my fabulous publicists, Sara Mercurio and Michelle Blankenship; and the warm and enthusiastic editors Helen Garnons-Williams and Nick Humphrey, the excellent publicist Jude Drake, and the rest of the Bloomsbury UK staff. And last but not least, Dale de la Torre, a beloved friend who has generously guided me in all things legal and ethical for many years. I am forever your grateful Grasshopper.

And finally, thank you to the original love junkie. Ma, I will always love you.